Radical Bear Hunter

Radical Bear Hunter

Dick Scorzafava

STACKPOLE
BOOKS

Published by
STACKPOLE BOOKS
5067 Ritter Road
Mechanicsburg, PA 17055
www.stackpolebooks.com

Printed in China

First edition

10 9 8 7 6 5 4 3 2 1

Cover design by Wendy A. Reynolds
Cover photograph by Rex Summerfield

Library of Congress Cataloging-in-Publication Data

Scorzafava, Dick.
  Radical bear hunter / Dick Scorzafava. — 1st ed.
     p. cm.
  Includes index.
  ISBN-13: 978-0-8117-3418-9
  ISBN-10: 0-8117-3418-8
  1. Black bear hunting. 2. Bear hunting. I. Title.

SK295.S385 2007
799.2′7784—dc22

                                                                    2006038363

Contents

Acknowledgments

I sincerely hope that by sharing my knowledge about bears in this book, your life may change for the better. Everyone who reads these pages can, given the proper mindset and effort, become a radical bear hunter and a responsible member of the hunting community as well.

I would like to send out my heartfelt thanks to my dad, who passed away while I was writing this book and who will never get to see the finished product. My dad was a very humble man who fished and hunted with me my entire life, and he was extremely proud of my accomplishments. He was my best buddy and I miss him, but I know he is watching over me from the heavens above.

It would be impossible to identify every person, manufacturer, or organization that in some way helped me in the creation of this book. No doubt I will miss someone in my efforts to name as many as possible. If so, please forgive me and know that your contribution was nonetheless much appreciated.

I am deeply grateful to outdoor writer Frank Sousa whose support helped launch my writing and speaking career. Frank has also done me the favor of writing the foreword for this book. I am privileged to be counted as one of his friends. Thanks for everything, Frank.

You will enjoy many of John Dziza's photographs that grace the pages of this book and add visual impact to my words. He is a master at his art and another guy I call friend. I continue to be grateful to my hunting and fishing pal (and marketing wizard) Walt Larsen, president of Scales Outdoor Group, for his continued support and guidance. Without friends such as these, this book would probably still be in the idea stage. Thanks in part to them, it has become a reality.

Thanks also to the following people who were particularly helpful and supportive not only in the research of this massive project, but because of their true friendships: Greg Sesselmann, president, and George Schrink, vice president, of Scent-Lok Technologies; Ron Bice of Wildlife Research Center; Matt McPherson, Joel Maxfield, and Mike Zieball of Mathews, Inc.; Mike Mattly of Knight Muzzleloaders; Mark Cuddeback of Non-Typical Inc.; Dave Larsen of Gamehide; Mike Ellig of Montana Black Gold; Larry Pulkrabek of Field Logic; Brooks Johnson and Keith Beam of Double Bull Blinds; Ken Byers of Byers Media; Deb Lazenby of Thorlo; Jeff Folsom, editor of *Bear Hunting Magazine;* and Pat Gorman of Integrated Safety.

Last but not least, I want to thank all the friends and family who have supported me through my many years of hunting black bears and who somehow in some way contributed to the writing of this book.

Foreword

If I had been an Indian chief and Dick Scorzafava had been born into my tribe, he would have been named Bear Talker. Or perhaps Listener to Bears.

In my fifty years as an outdoors editor and writer, many outdoorsmen have come under my eye-of-the-hawk scrutiny, and when it comes to bear hunting, a certain number, I would venture to say, have actually appeared to understand our largest of predators. Fewer, yet, however, have understood that each bear is an individual, with its own traits and a power to pulverize, a very wild thing, indeed. The black bear has an innate ability to play hide and seek, with its life the prize. And quite possibly, under certain conditions, the hunter, or the innocent who thinks real bears are plaything Paddingtons, can become the hunted.

The bear hunter must know that to get a bear within his or her grasp, one must get cunningly close to his or her adversary, which has one of the strongest, sharpest grasps in the world. To think of a bruin as anything but an adversary is a big-time mistake. When hunting for bear, you truly have an opponent, more so than when seeking any other North American big game.

A few years ago, *National Geographic* produced a special on black bears that said the animal was responsible for more run-ins with humans nearing ruination than any other species in the bear family. This finding is not mentioned here to frighten you. To the contrary, in this book, Dick Scorzafava presents teachings that will make you more—rather than less—confident around bears. Because with learning comes confidence.

Whether you're a beginner who wants to be introduced to bear hunting or an experienced hunter who wants to bring the bruiser bruin into closer range, you will do well to go to the top of the hunting pyramid for a mentor, one who has learned from the mistakes and absorbed the abilities of those who make up the bulk of the triangle. Every type of hunter can learn from the teachings, experiences, and expertise of the best.

While I'm certainly not a fan of Disney's *Bambi*, I did derive part of my life philosophy from bit player Thumper, the rabbit, whose mother told him, "If you can't say something nice, don't say anything at all." So although over the years I have endorsed several experts on deer hunting, I had never found an expert on bear hunting that I could stand behind. That is until I came across one who comes as close to being able to talk with bears without actually being a bear. This Bear Talker has written the book you are now holding that I consider to be the definitive word on bear hunting.

Dick is a self-taught man who has earned what I call the three major degrees. His first degree in bear biology was learned by both reading books and tramping the woods with experts and biologists in the field. A second degree was earned while spending many hours looking down a rifle, shotgun, muzzleloader, handgun, and bow. To attain the third degree, he had to pay his dues at—where else?—the School of Hard Knocks.

With an integrity not found in all how-to authors, he admits that part of his education was formed by making mistakes. To his everlasting credit, he reports that much is to be learned from mistakes, but if you listen to what he has to tell you, you don't have to make the same errors.

Dick didn't enter the woods and fields as a teenager looking for an escape from computers, TV, and electronic games. His father was one of thirteen children who quickly learned that if the family was to have meat on the table, he had to be a successful hunter. Dick was about eight when he started hunting rabbits, squirrels, and chipmunks—all big game to a kid. Learning to hit something small and to think like a small animal when you're a kid certainly helps when later in life you plan to think like big game and down big game.

And big game he did down. The 6-foot 8-inch bear he shot in Idaho in the spring of 2006 wasn't shabby, but then he took things to the next level when one month later, in Manitoba, he shot a 7-foot 8-inch bear with an estimated weight of nearly 600 pounds. It had a green score of $22^2/16$, which would put it in the top ten of black bears of all time. But most likely, this bear will not make the record books because Dick is not a record seeker. Rather, he is a bear hunter, who travels within his Bay State backyard and as far away as the Arctic expanse in search of bruins.

Bear Talker's first up close encounter with a big bear resulted in a roar and an "Oh, my God!" It occurred while he was tranquilizing bears, taking down health statistics, and putting monitors on them with a crew of biologists. While he was lugging a supposedly tranquilized bear out of a tree, the bruin gained consciousness, opened its maw, some 6 inches from Dick's face, and roared. What Dick remembers most from this encounter was not his heart standing still, but rather that the bruin's breath was putrid.

"But this didn't keep me from realizing these great animals are intelligent, with some having unusual intelligence," he told me. "And all are individuals." Hey, bears even come in a variety of colors: blond, chocolate, cinnamon, black and white, and basic black.

Many who live close to bears regard them with great respect, and Dick found, starting with our Native Americans, the Inuits of the far north and other early groups, that many people hold them in reverence. He said that on an isolated island off the coast of British Columbia, they have a bear, known as the Spirit Bear, that appears to be a throwback to the ice age.

As paradoxical as it may seem to some, Dick is dedicated to ensuring that bears have a future in what is quickly becoming a man-only world. But in respecting this awesome creature, he also seeks to help both the beginner and experienced hunter get the biggest bear of his or her life.

Bear need habitat, food, game law protection, and the expertise of biologists, Dick said, but they also need humans to understand them, especially as the bruin population expands into the suburbs, often in close proximity to man. When this happens, of course, humans must be kept safe. This safety must come through education by learning that the supposedly docile bear is not a Paddington and thus deserves our respect. "People must understand that a fed bear is a dead bear," he said. "They are not tame and must never be tamed."

Dick Scorzafava is the first writer of a bear book to touch all the bases after hitting a home run. He is truly both the Bear Talker and the Listener of Bears.

Frank Sousa
Editor/Publisher, *Woods and Waters USA*

Introduction

A hunter who chooses to bear hunt has already upped the ante. By deciding to hunt a black bear, he can ascend to another level. He can leave his safe existence behind for a few hours or days and enter into a new realm of excitement and potential danger. The exhilaration of black bear hunting is unparalleled. These creatures of the forest are a unique species to hunt: Their size, strength, and speed make them a formidable adversary. But black bears are not docile prey animals that will bolt off to safety; rather, they can be a fierce predator who kills to eat and who can and will charge and attack a human.

This book is meant not only to share my many years of experience studying and hunting these magnificent creatures all over the North American continent, but to inform readers of the various methods of hunting black bears, some of which they may not have tried or even considered, and to provide techniques, tips, strategies, and equipment suggestions that have worked well for me. For your reading enjoyment, I share some trophy harvesting experiences and a few close encounters with the black bear. Consider that more encounters occur each year with black bears than any other type of bear, and the numbers are growing annually.

Black bear hunting can enrich and extend your time in the woods since many areas offer two bear seasons, spring and fall. Due to the nature of some of the methods and the location you select for your bear hunt, you may also be able to enjoy world-class fishing or have a combination hunt.

This radical bear hunter will share his many years of experience hunting the black bear and will teach those who wish to pursue this majestic big-game animal how to do it radically. So if you aspire to ascend to the higher level of hunter, read on and become a radical bear hunter like me.

CHAPTER 1

The Beginning of My Love Affair with the Bear

The most important part of being a good hunter is gaining an intricate knowledge of your quarry. When it comes to black bears, I've been fortunate to have had a whole lifetime to learn about this fascinating species. Black bears have excited me ever since the day my dad pulled a stuffed toy bear out of a box for my sixth birthday. The toy had a cord on its back, and when you pulled it, the bear growled. From that moment on, I was hooked and destined to become a bear hunter.

Few creatures in North America will inspire more awe and respect than a black bear. It symbolizes the true spirit of the wilderness and is a central figure in history and mythology. The drawings by the Native people and their legends, the adventures and exploits of the fur traders, and tall tales from game wardens, explorers, and hunters have added to our fascination with the "black ghost of the forest." The black bear is the type of bear that people most often encounter in the wild. Across the North American range, they number well over seven hundred thousand and are many more times abundant than the other species of bears.

The black bear can be extremely dangerous to humans. I bet you didn't know that black bears are the most likely bear to stalk, kill, and even eat you. Most of them do not know they are supposed to be afraid of humans. To them, everything that moves in the woods is a potential meal, and they will stalk you, believe me! Just check the records on human attacks by a black bear; it will open your eyes.

RUNNING WITH THE HOUNDS

I grew up running behind beagle hounds with my dad, and later I got into running first-class bear hounds. It was a great time of my life. Back then, there were no restrictions, and we could run our hounds at any time in my home state of Massachusetts. The hounds, I believe, really enjoyed

Plott hounds treed on a bear in Massachusetts during the early years.

the excitement of the pursuit, even more than I did. To me, there is nothing more exciting than listening to the chop squall voices of a good pack of Plott hounds on the hot trail of a big bear. The thrill of the chase with the hounds providing a symphony of background music can really get my adrenaline flowing.

I have hunted black bears using every legal method—baiting, spot and stalk, and hunting with hounds—and although the other methods can be very productive, running behind an impressive pack of hounds is both demanding and exciting as hell. Having hunted black bears from Alaska to Newfoundland, I know that other methods can be more productive given the right scenario, but running the hounds will always be close to my heart.

Glory Years in Canada
Each spring for several years, during the early 1970s, I would hook up with fellow bear hunting fanatics and head off to a remote area just above Lake Nipigon in the Canadian province of Ontario. Back then, this area was virtually untouched by bear hunters, and some really monster bears

This large Canadian bear bayed on the ground for over twelve hours before we were able to get close enough for a killing shot.

This young hound learned a valuable lesson about porcupines that day.

Canadian bear taken during the autumn of '78.

roamed around in the biggest cedar swamps imaginable. With no limit on the number of bears you could bag, one just had to go into the Department of Natural Resources office and purchase another license for a nominal fee. If I recollect correctly, I believe it was five dollars. Because of the large concentration of bears that were in this area, this was a great location to run young, inexperienced hounds with the old pros. By culling out the hounds that would not meet our standards, we could put the best pack together in a very short period of time.

The area was huge with only a few logging roads running through it so it was difficult to cut off the hounds by using any kind of road. You had to get into the bush and try to keep up with the hounds. The bears would always head into the biggest, thickest cedar swamps, which were nearly impossible for us to get through, never mind trying to keep up with the hounds. We had some long chases in that country, and many bears would never tree. The dogs would continually bay up on the ground, and the bear would fight with the dogs for a while and then be off running again. It was almost as if the bear had stopped to rest and the dogs were like flies that it would try to swat away. The old hounds were on to those tricks and would take turns biting the bear on the butt while others barked in his face. When he turned around to try to swat the dogs biting him, the ones barking in his face then would bite him on the butt.

The young dogs learned quickly that they had to stay out of reach of the bear or they would get hooked up with his claws. These situations would always get my heart hammering. When running into one of these scenes on the ground, it became close encounters of the dangerous kind. One never knew if the bear would just charge and pounce on one of the hunters.

At the time, this area had more bears than anywhere I had ever been. In fact, there were so many bears that they were putting a lot of pressure on the moose herd, especially the calves in the spring. A biologist in the area told us that bears had caused almost a seventy-five percent mortality rate on calves, and with no one hunting the bears it was getting worse. After we heard that, we decided to take as many bears as we could during our visits in an effort to keep the bears in check. I remember one week when our group shot thirteen bears, several of which were what anyone would consider a trophy bear.

WORKING WITH BIOLOGISTS

As a young man, I had the opportunity to learn a lot about black bears through my state bear biologist. During the late 1970s, I spent thousands of hours with the biologist collecting data to monitor population

One of thirteen bears harvested on our Canadian hunt during my early days of black bear hunting with the hounds.

Treed bear in Massachusetts that was tranquilized, collared with a telemetry unit, and tagged for monitoring.

levels, the age structure, and the reproductive parameters of sows. The sows were typically radio-collared while in their winter dens, and their movements outside hibernation were monitored. I remember the first time I crawled on my belly into a bear's den to tranquilize a sow so that we could change her telemetry collar and conduct a physical on her and her cubs. I was both excited and scared as I crept through the dark cover with a small flashlight in my mouth to try to spot the sow and stick her with the tranquilizer. This is the kind of experience that takes getting used to, even when you are young and fearless.

We also used culvert traps to entrap and hounds to tree bears so that we could tag and collar the bears, either for further studies or when a bear was creating a problem in an area. The state needed sound data on which to base quality management decisions regarding the bears. Good research can help alleviate bear problems. For example, the information

Both bears were harvested on the same day during the late 1970s: one in Vermont, the other in New Hampshire.

we gathered proved that hunting does not have a negative impact on the overall bear population. As a matter of fact, in my home state of Massachusetts the bear population has grown substantially, despite an increase in hunting, from approximately a hundred animals back in the early 1970s to more than twenty-five hundred animals in 2005.

Some of the increase in the bear population could be traced to the state's elimination of hunting with hounds several years ago. Most of the people who voted this into law do not have to deal with the bear problems that people in the western end of the state have to face. Most likely the only place that people from the eastern end of the state have ever seen a bear is in the zoo, if at all, and they have no idea what problems these animals can cause and how much money it costs the state to correct them.

THE RADICAL BEAR HUNTER

Back in the early 1980s, I teamed up with several fellow bear hunters to guide hound and bait hunts where legal in New England, Ontario, and British Columbia. When we weren't guiding clients on hunts, we were hunting black bears ourselves, moving from coast to coast to follow the hunting seasons. During those years, I witnessed some incredible things in the wild, and in one season I had more bear encounters than most

Massachusetts bear harvested by author Dick Scorzafava during the early hound season.

experienced hunters have in a lifetime of hunts. This intense level of experience has transformed me into a radical bear hunter, and I continue to actively hunt black bears every year.

Over the years I spent hunting these ghosts of the forest, I have experienced every legal hunting method possible. I have hunted these magnificent creatures in almost every state or Canadian province that allows black bear hunting, and I have killed more than a hundred bears while guiding or being part of a group during very close to nine hundred harvests. That's a lot of years and a lot of bears. My goal in writing this book is to give every bear hunter the knowledge that will transform him or her into a radical bear hunter.

To become a radical bear hunter, you must make a serious commitment on your part to master the skills and tactics necessary to realize your full potential for harvesting whopper black bears. So forget about the luck factor and throw out all the old-fashioned lessons you've learned about black bear hunting over the years. If you want to kill those big old monster bruins, you will have to start thinking differently.

This book will show you:
- How to find big black bear hot spots in North America
- How to field judge a good black bear
- How to read bear sign
- The right questions to ask a prospective outfitter
- Do-it-yourself bear hunting
- Special techniques for bear hunting outside the box
- How to take advantage of the latest and greatest equipment to get the overall job done

If you have dreamed of taking a trophy black bear and are ready to step up to the next level, this book will teach you all the necessary skills. The bear of your dreams will test the full range of your skills and transform you into a radical bear hunter. By putting all of your new knowledge to use, you will be able to achieve the ultimate victory—a trophy bear.

CHAPTER 2

Understanding the Black Bear

To become a radical bear hunter, you first must understand the population and distribution of the black bear. This information will enable you to better pinpoint locations for the best hunting opportunities. You also need to know about the anatomy of the black bear, the size of the black bear, and the senses of the black bear. Once you learn these things, you can determine the perfect shot placement for a clean quick kill or quickly assess the size of the animal so you know almost immediately whether he is the trophy you are after.

The size of bears varies, and many will tell you they are the most difficult of all game animals to determine size. Of all the big-game animals in North America, bears have the most ground shrinkage, and let's face it, when estimating a bear's size you don't want to make a mistake, since this is not a catch and release sport. Thoroughly understanding a bear's senses will enable you to overcome them when you want to get up close and personal without the bear being aware of your presence. Knowing the basic groundwork will help a hunter understand his quarry before entering into the bear woods to hunt. My goal with this chapter is to lay the groundwork so that you better understand the black ghost of the forest.

DISTRIBUTION AND POPULATION

The black bear *(Ursus americanus)* is endemic to North America, which means that it is only found on this one continent and nowhere else in the world. Because beans are very adaptive in their nature, they are distributed across the entire continent of North America, from Alaska to Mexico. Prior to European colonization, the black bear was found throughout the entire continent of North America except in the very arid desert regions of the Southwest and the barren tundra areas of Canada. The black bear once inhabited all of our fifty states, except Hawaii, and thrived throughout all twelve of Canada's provinces. Today, however, the black bear is extinct in the province of Prince Edward Island, and its numbers are threatened in the states of Alabama, Connecticut, Delaware, Illinois, Indiana, Iowa, Kansas, Nebraska, Rhode Island, South Dakota, and Texas.

Only twenty-seven states in the United States and eleven of the twelve Canadian provinces have substantial populations of black bears and a hunting season today. In Mexico, the black bear is endangered, and the hunting season has been closed since 1985. Yet the Mexican government continues to have trouble controlling the poaching of these magnificent animals.

Determining the number of black bears present in a given region can be difficult. The black bear is too secretive, wide ranging, and tough to catch without harming it to make an accurate count even possible. For those reasons, wildlife managers use what is called an estimate or population estimate to approximate the true population based on some sampling methods.

In my past work performing studies with biologists, it was difficult to get data for population studies in areas of heavy forested habitat. We

An Alaska black bear fishing in a stream during the fall salmon run.

·d it by radio-collaring and handling large numbers of bears, 1 methods put extreme stress on the animals. Recent advances .:chnology through DNA testing have enabled biologists to determine individuals, gender, and species from hair and feces samples without ever touching a bear. The population density can be easily and accurately estimated from hair collected at a strategically placed hair trap.

Several years ago a bear study in western Canada showed that adult males can affect the bear population when they evict or kill younger males and, to a much lesser degree, females. The four-year study concluded that removing adult males through hunting increased survival rates of the younger males and females. Such information proved that the adult males regulated the population density by controlling recruitment of the younger immature males.

In the northern United States and Canada, female bears that eat only wild natural foods have a lower reproductive rate and mature much more slowly than a female that is able to supplement her diet with other foods such as fish or garbage. In the state of Pennsylvania where high-energy mast crops are available to the bears for much longer in the year than in the north, the female bears mature much more quickly and reproduce at an age of three to four years (compared to six and a half years for the northern bears). The food supply in an area is a major factor determining population densities of bear. For bears to thrive in an area, the habitat has to provide abundant, reliable, and well-distributed food in the spring, summer, and fall. A steady food supply will increase the growth rate of bears, decrease the age of female first reproduction, and enhance cub survival.

The population density of the black bear varies widely across the North American range with the highest numbers in Alaska, where estimates of a hundred fifty thousand animals have been determined. The Pacific Northwest in the Canadian province of British Columbia has an estimated population of a hundred forty thousand black bears. The latest estimates of black bears living across the entire North American range are nine hundred sixty-six thousand and growing. When you compare this number to the estimated half-million bears living across the continent when the settlers arrived from Europe, the total population of black bears has grown since colonial times even though their historic range has shrunk dramatically. It's not unheard of to find high population densities of thirty-five to forty bears per hundred square miles, or even a little higher, in exceptional hunting areas such as those around Lynn Lake in Manitoba and Prince of Wales Island in Alaska.

ESTIMATED BLACK BEAR POPULATIONS IN THE UNITED STATES AND CANADA

State/Province	Population	State/Province	Population
Alaska	140,000	Rhode Island	10
Arizona	2,500	South Carolina	600
Arkansas	3,500	Tennessee	2,500
California	33,000	Texas	50
Colorado	11,000	Utah	3,000
Connecticut	125	Vermont	4,500
Georgia	1,900	Virginia	8,000
Idaho	20,000	Washington	10,000
Maine	24,000	West Virginia	11,000
Maryland	600	Wisconsin	13,000
Massachusetts	2,500	Wyoming	10,000
Michigan	18,000		
Minnesota	24,000	**CANADA**	
Mississippi	50	Alberta	35,000
Missouri	150	British Columbia	140,000
Montana	17,000	Manitoba	30,000
New Hampshire	6,000	New Brunswick	17,000
New Jersey	1,500	Newfoundland/	
New Mexico	5,000	Labrador	90,000
New York	7,000	NW Territories	10,000
North Carolina	11,000	Nova Scotia	10,000
North Dakota	10	Ontario	90,000
Ohio	25	Quebec	70,000
Oregon	27,500	Saskatchewan	30,000
Pennsylvania	15,000	Yukon	10,000
		TOTAL	**966,020**

Source: Bear Hunting Magazine

BEAR ANATOMY

We as hunters have an ethical responsibility when hunting black bears to make a clean, quick kill and to recover the game that we shoot. How many times have you heard someone complain about all the hunters who wound game and never recover the animal? The anti-hunters just love this stuff. If we don't quickly kill and recover our game, we are adding fuel to the fire and helping the anti-hunter get sympathy from the general public in their efforts to close hunting seasons down. The keys to a clean, quick kill and recovery of your black bear are accurate shot placement, shooting within your ability, and understanding the anatomy of the black bear so you will know where to place the shot with your weapon of choice.

The black bear has a much heavier bone structure and hide than most other big-game animals. Not only are they significantly different in their structure, but bears are also potentially much larger in size. The skeleton of a black bear is designed for power and strength. They have massive shoulders, very thick limbs, and a short back, which is why they are not an efficient predator. Their skulls are massive and larger than most other big-game animals on the North American continent, and the hinge of their jawbone is large to accommodate the heavy muscles of the jaw. The average bear's skull is $6^1/2$ inches wide and $11^1/2$ inches long. A sow's skull is narrower and much more pointed than that of a mature boar. A black bear has forty-two teeth that are normally in place by the time they reach 2 and a half years of age. The teeth are large and omnivorous with incisors, canines, premolars, and molars. Black bears use their premolars and molars for grinding their food, and their teeth, when used in combination with their paws and claws, are their first-line tools in obtaining food and defending themselves.

Knowing these facts, you will want to have the right shot placement on a black bear to ensure a quick, clean, efficient kill and to recover the animal. In my opinion, the black bear is one of, if not *the*, most difficult big-game animal to judge where to place that killing shot. A wounded black bear is difficult and sometimes almost impossible to track because the animal's layers of body fat and long dense fur often soak up most or all of the blood before it can drip on the ground and leave a trail to follow. Keep in mind that a wounded black bear could attack and, far from an exciting adventure, could turn a hunt into a life-threatening encounter. Back in my guiding days, I had several run-ins with bears wounded by clients. Believe me when I say that an angry bear is bad enough to deal with, but facing an angry, pain-crazed, wounded bear can be harrowing and intimidating to even the pros. If a hunter panics, drops his gun,

The anatomy of the black bear.

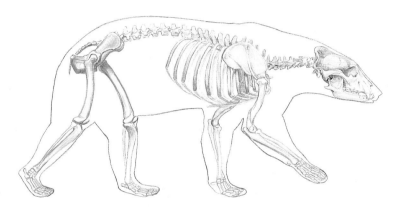

Black bear's skeletal system.

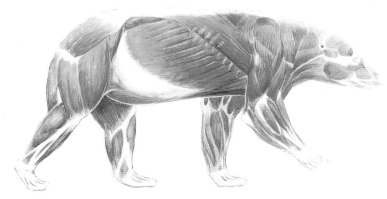

Musculature of the black bear.

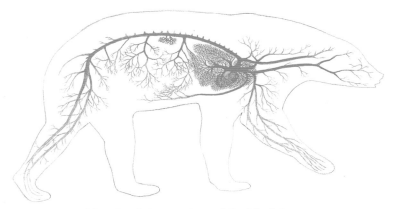

The circulatory system of the black bear.

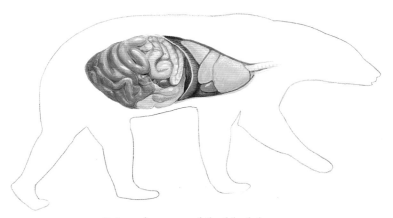

Internal organs of the black bear.

freezes, or runs, he has lost whatever advantage he might have had over this awesome bear, and he is in serious jeopardy.

A bowhunter uses a razor-sharp broadhead on the tip of his arrow to cut the bear's flesh, arteries, and veins, and if the shot placement is correct, this will result in severe blood loss. An arrow can easily cut through the soft bones on the rib cage of a black bear but will rarely, if ever, penetrate the heavy bones of a bear's hips, head, neck, and shoulders. The bowhunter's perfect shot every time should be a spot in the middle of the lungs from a broadside position. This shot will not only result in massive bleeding, but it will cause the bear's lungs to collapse, and a quick death through suffocation to result. Because the lungs on a bear are quite large, they make a sizable target. Also, other vital organs surround them: A bear's heart is between the lungs, and the aortic artery is on the top of the heart; the liver and kidneys are on the back of the lungs, and the spine goes just below the top of their back.

Bear hunters using a firearm have more choices on the shots they can take, but a bullet shot into the heart, lungs, shoulder, or spine areas will result in massive shock and tissue destruction and will prove fatal to a black bear. Many bullets today have the design, speed, and weight to smash through the heaviest bones of a bear and enter into the vital organs.

The bear hunter using a smokepole or muzzleloader has to make special consideration to shot placement because the heavy bullet has less down-range energy than a center-fire rifle bullet. In most situations when using a muzzleloader, you will only get one shot off because of the time it takes to reload the weapon. Any bear hunter using a muzzleloader should only shoot within their own effective range, which should not be more than 100 yards. The bear hunter's top priority once he decides to take the bear should be to make a clean, quick kill on the animal. This requires keen marksmanship skills, a true shooting weapon, and the patience to wait for the perfect shot angle. For any firearm bear hunter, this would be a broadside shot, although the quartering-away broadside, quartering-toward, and head-on shots are effective with a firearm large enough for black bear.

The bear hunter should study the anatomy of the black bear and practice enough to be able to make clean, one-shot kills with their weapon of choice when the opportunity arises. Thoroughly understanding the anatomy of the black bear will enable the hunter to make a quick killing shot, which should be every bear hunter's goal.

SIZE

The size of the black bear is normally expressed in terms of the animal's weight. Most black bear hunters and the general public often misjudge the weight of the black bear. While black bears can be very large, they are not the 1,000-pound monsters they are made out to be from the people who encounter them in the wild. I can't tell you how many times people have told me about the bear they saw last fall that had to be well over 1,000 pounds. To the untrained eye, all bears are huge, often much greater than their actual size. From my experiences, most people estimate a bear's weight at at least twice the actual weight of the animal. Because bears are perceived to be ferocious toward humans, they often appear much larger than they actually are. Like the old saying goes, perception is reality. I have always joked with people at my seminars by telling them the farther they get a black bear away from a scale, the more it will weigh.

The actual weight of a bear depends on many factors, including the age, health, and sex of the animal, the season of year, the bear's individual ability to locate food or digest a specific food, and the condition of the habitat. The seasonal fluctuations of a black bear's weight are very predictable. In the fall of the year, their pre-den weight is normally about thirty percent higher than their spring emergence weight. Their weight can also be affected by food sources available during the different seasons of the year. Also, it is important to note that the black bears on the East Coast of North America are on average heavier than those found on the West Coast. The male black bear is generally thirty-three percent bigger in overall size than a sow of the same age, and this differential is caused by what is called sexual dimorphism.

To obtain the weight of black bears, harvested animals are weighed at checking stations during hunting seasons, and when they are immobilized for management research. The heaviest black bear ever recorded was a male that weighed 880 pounds and was ten and three-quarter years old when he was harvested in North Carolina in the late 1990s. In 2001, a vehicle traveling near Winnipeg, Manitoba, hit a monster boar that tipped the scales at 886 pounds. The average male black bear weighs 225 pounds, but their weight ranges from 125 pounds to over 550 pounds. Females are much smaller with an average weight of 125 pounds and a range of between 90 and 275 pounds.

A mature black bear male will measure between $2^1/2$ to 3 feet tall from the bottom of the paw when flat on the ground to the high point on the shoulders. The overall length of a mature boar will average around 5 feet, from the tip of its nose to the tip of its tail.

SENSES

Recent studies show that the black bear has reasonably good eyesight. Although there is still much to learn about the visual capabilities of the black bear, several biologists believe that a bear acts as if it has poor vision because it doesn't trust its eyes as well as it trusts its superior nose. The black bear's eyes are small, round, various shades of brown, widely spaced, and facing forward. Black bears also have the ability to see colors and are particularly sensitive to blue, red, and green wavelengths. Since a large part of their diet consists of different colored berries and fruits, this sensitivity to color helps them to find food. The nearsighted black bear has difficulty trying to distinguish objects at any great distance, but its binocular vision allows the bear very good depth perception. Like most other nocturnal animals, the black bear's eyes are reflective and mirror the faintest glow of the moon. The eye's reflective layer, called tarpetum lucidum, which lines the back of the eyeball, allows the eye to reflect light back through the retina to stimulate the rods for a second time and greatly improve the bear's night vision.

Because we are unable to test a bear's hearing to obtain positive results like we do for humans, it is very difficult to determine how well a bear can actually hear. But from the data that is available, most researchers believe that a black bear can hear somewhere between 16 and 20 megahertz, and quite possibly higher in the ultrasonic range. A bear's ear structure is unique compared to any other carnivore. Its middle ear has a bony structure shaped like a balloon that forms a resonating chamber around its eardrum. These structures, called the auditory bullae, increase a bear's hearing sensitivity. A black bear's hearing does not play a prominent role in its daily activities and is not nearly as reliable as its sense of sight or as keen as its incredible sense of smell, but hunters would be wise to remember that a black bear can hear at least as well as, if not better than, any human.

The black bear's most important sense is its smell. No other animal in the entire animal kingdom has a keener sense of smell. It allows a bear to locate a mate, avoid other bears, identify its cubs, and find a food source. Although the region of the black bear's brain that is devoted to sense of smell is only average size, the area of nasal mucous membrane in its head is a hundred times bigger in size than a human's. An organ in the roof of a bear's mouth called a Jacobson's organ further enhances its sense of smell. To put this in perspective for you, a black bear has a sense of smell seven times better than a bloodhound, and everyone knows how well one of them can sniff out something. A bear cub learns the smell of food items by sniffing the mouth of its mother. Although not tested and proven, it is widely believed that a black bear can identify the dead carcass of an animal from several miles away. A black bear in northern California was once observed traveling in a straight line upwind three miles to reach the carcass of a dead Columbian black-tailed deer.

As do all animals, including humans, the black bear has a very distinct odor. This odor is quite pronounced, though not necessarily repugnant depending on an individual's nose, and I believe it is the easiest scent for a dog to track. Once you have experienced the odor of a bear, you will never forget it. When you smell the odor again, you will know instantly it's a bear.

The animal's habitats, habits, and physical characteristics all come into play when you are trying to learn about the black bear. A radical bear hunter will learn as much as possible about his prey before entering into the woods, and once in those woods will use each experience to understand more about this formidable adversary.

CHAPTER 3

Reading Bear Sign

Compared to a white-tailed deer, a black bear, especially a large mature boar, has a much larger home range than most hunters realize. For the hunter, this means a lot less sign to look for so you better be good at reading the sign you see. Because a radical bear hunter knows what to look for, he can dramatically increase his odds of finding a bear. An average mature boar's home range is more than ten square miles and can be as large as sixty square miles, depending on the habitat in the region. Find a bear scratch tree, which indicates where mature boars' territories overlap, and you've just doubled your odds for success.

Regardless of how you choose to hunt your black bear, you want to be sure you are hunting in an area that is inhabited by at least one bear. To actually see a bear in the wild is by far the most reliable way to verify that an animal is in the hunting area. Unfortunately, black bears are very secretive in nature. This fact, combined with the dense heavy cover and rugged terrain they usually occupy, makes sighting a bear nearly impossible. In most cases, the bear hunter must rely on reading whatever signs the bears have left in the area. These signs can give a radical bear hunter plenty of information about the color, size, sex, feeding habits, general behavior, and even breeding status of the black bears in any particular area he plans to hunt.

Several years ago, this radical bear hunter was on a spring hunt at a fly-in camp east of Fort McMurray in the Canadian province of Alberta with an outfitter friend named Jeff Dodds. Jeff had six baits that were not hunted during the entire season, and he told me I could select the one that looked best to me. I spent an entire day carefully examining each bait site for its trophy bear potential and discovered that all six of the baits had been hit, with two totally cleaned out. I decided on a bait location Jeff had named Raven after his operation, Raven Outfitters LTD. It was located over five miles from an old dirt road in an area with thick, dense spruce trees that ended along the banks of an almost impenetrable bug-infested cedar swamp. Even on a clear blue-sky day, the area was quite dark, the kind of spot that a big mature boar likes but that will send a chill down your back when you are stalking through it.

We put up another treestand along the edge of the swamp to take advantage of the light from above and to position myself so I could ambush any big boy on his way to the bait. After deciding to hunt this spot the following evening, we returned to camp and fished for an hour before a late dinner.

The next evening, I positioned myself on the stand and settled in for almost five hours of absolutely no action at all. I was just about to give up for the night when with about a half hour of shooting light left, I heard something coming at me from the swamp. Suddenly, as if on cue, a huge bruin appeared in front of me, approaching the bait without a bit of hesitation. What a monster! He was almost as wide as he was long, and his belly seemed to drag on the ground as he slowly moved toward the bait area. Slowly and carefully I drew my bow, anchored, picked a spot just behind his shoulder, and released the arrow as he passed within ten yards of my treestand. Almost instantly I heard the "thunk" of the hit and watched the yellow vanes disappear into his rib cavity. It was a perfect hit. He leaped straight into the air like an acrobat jumping on a trampoline and bolted approximately twenty yards before piling up in a big heap, out of my sight. The woods went stone quiet as my heart started pounding so loudly I could hear it with my ears. I knew there would be no ground shrinkage with this bear. Any bowhunter would agree that he was truly the kind of bear that dreams are made of. We could never weigh the big old boar, but we estimated he was well over 400 pounds. He had a $20^{12}/_{16}$-inch skull. Now that is what this radical bear hunter calls a real whopper bear, especially for the spring.

How did I know which bait to hunt and that the bait was being hit by an old mature bruin? Most hunters would have picked one of the other baits that looked like they were hit much harder; at first glance they did appear to offer the best opportunity to harvest a bear. However, I read the bear sign available at each bait site and analyzed the data to determine the best possible location to kill a big bear. All the other baits had been hit every night, and one was especially torn up with bear sign everywhere. After thoroughly examining the bait at this active site, I determined a sow with cubs was hitting it. Young cubs will run over a feed area, crushing and disturbing the vegetation, tearing up any dead leaves and dirt, and making a total mess. You must always look at the big picture when examining an area to hunt. By doing some investigation and ground work first, you can determine the best location to spend your time to harvest the bear of your dreams.

The fastest way to learn how to interpret black bear sign is by reading all the concentrated bear sign available at a bait site, whether it's one set up by you or an outfitter. Like a crime scene investigator, you must study and analyze all the sign available around that area and then carefully and correctly put together the puzzle.

If the hunter actually sees a big black bear and can accurately judge its size, then he has the most reliable way to determine if a big old boar is in the area he plans to hunt. Understanding what to look for and being able to actually determine the size of the bears is critical if you want to consistently kill monster bears.

TRACKS
Bear hunters usually get excited when they see a bear track in the woods, but the track itself only accounts for about ten percent of the total calling cards a bear leaves behind. A hunter who can read bear sign, including tracks, can tell where, when, and what a bear is eating and can determine the size and sex of a bear.

The black bear is a wide-bodied animal called a pacer that moves both legs on the same side of its body at a time. Like humans, bears are plantigrade walkers, which means the heel on their back foot will land flat on the ground with each step they take. The trail width of a black bear, measured between the outer edges of the footprints, is on average 14 inches. The average stride of a black bear is 18 to 19 inches if the animal is walking and will grow to 2 to 5 feet, depending on its speed, when it is on the run. The stride is easily measured from the tip of the leading toe on one foot to the tip of the same toe on the other foot.

A bear's flat, large foot does not easily make deep impressions in soil, unless the ground is soft, moist, muddy, or snow-covered or the animal is running. But among other animal tracks, a bear's are easy to recognize. The rear print looks much like a human bare footprint with five toes on each foot, except that the big toe of a bear is on the outside of its foot as opposed to a human's big toe on the inside of the foot. Because of that, a bear's little toe does not always show in a track. The claw marks will be ahead of the toes but often do not show in the track. The front paws leave a print similar to a human's without the heel or the instep area. In the typical walking pattern, the hind foot of the bear will overstep its forefoot. A set of tracks closely followed by a smaller set indicates a sow with a cub.

You also can determine how large a bear is by the size of its track. When measuring a bear track, only take the pad into account, discounting

The average stride of a black bear shown in tracks found on a sandy beach.

Below: The front paw of a bear leaves a print similar to a human's without the heel or instep area.

This front paw measured just over 6 inches, which is representative of an exceptional and mature boar.

The rear pad from the same boar measured 7¹/₂ inches. CUDDEBACK DIGITAL

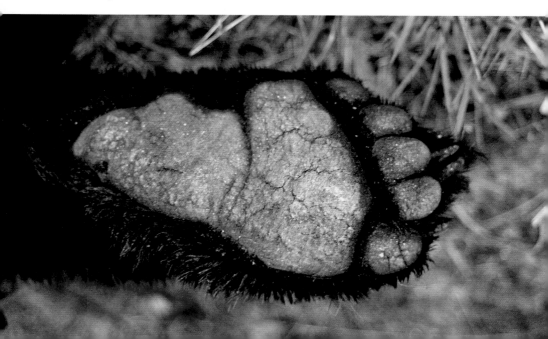

the toes and claws if visible. The average black bear in North America will have a rear pad that measures between 5 and 6 inches in total length. A bear with a rear pad of 7 inches or longer will be a real monster. The front pads of an average bear will be between $3^1/2$ and $4^1/2$ inches across the pad. If you find a track indicating a front pad that is 5 or more inches, you have come across the tracks of a mature boar. Anything over 6 inches across will be the kind of bear every hunter dreams about harvesting.

TRAILS
A trail made by bears can be a well-worn path used to cross another path or road or to enter a field to feed. Such trails become apparent when bears are using a concentrated food source, such as cornfields, baits, dumps, or landfills. Many times a bear will step in the tracks of the bear there before it. In fact, a trail that is used by a heavyweight bear will develop deep depressions because a black bear tends to step in the same spots each time it uses the trail. You may need a discerning eye to pick out a bear trail. This is not as easy as it sounds, but a soft leaf-covered area of ground will show patterns of footfalls, as eventually will a trail blazed across a grassy area. The bear hunter must be careful to distinguish this type of sign, especially when it's set against a backdrop lush with vegetation. Another sign to look out for is where a bear tunnels through a thicket at a height of approximately three feet from the ground.

DROPPINGS OR SCAT
Bears are regular eating machines, and their droppings are an evident and reliable source of their activity. Bear scat is usually found in large piles and will normally be black, brown, or white in color, depending on what the bears are feeding on at the time. The droppings rarely appear fresh for more than a day or two, unless the outside temperature is very cold.

The color and consistency of the stool reflects a bear's main food source. In the spring when grasses make up the major portion of a bear's diet, the droppings are dark green and resemble small, green, shredded-wheat squares with pieces of grass readily seen. When the droppings are dark brown or black, the bear has switched from a vegetarian diet and has been eating meat. When a bear has devoured hordes of ants, the scat will be black with evidence of sawdust. The droppings may look like a heap of fruit skins and seeds when fruit and berries are available. Bears that pig out on corn will produce stools with corn kernels clearly discernible. The condition and appearance of the dropping pile can give clues to how fresh the sign is. If the scat looks dry and white in color, it is old and starting to decay.

The color and visible remains of fruit skins indicate that the bear who left these droppings had been dining on berries.

The droppings deposited by a black bear in the wild are very characteristic and not likely to be mistaken for droppings left by any other big-game animal. The only exception would be in locations where the range of the grizzly bear overlaps that of the black bear. Black bear droppings contain clues that can lead an astute hunter to where the bear is feeding. Fresh droppings containing grass, berries, nuts, buds, bark, leaves, and roots reveal that the black bear is mostly a vegetarian. Droppings that contain other common black bear foods such as insects from rotten logs or stumps, mice, squirrels, beaver, and fish indicate whether the bear is finding its food in the woods or by water. I remember learning years ago that black bears will eat anything even if it is nailed down. As evidence, I have seen the droppings of bears that visit dumps contain such unusual items as batteries, tin cans, zippers, and pizza boxes.

The diameter of black bear droppings usually indicates the size of the bear that deposited them. If, for example, you find droppings of an average size alongside small droppings, you can bet a sow with cubs is in the area. As a general rule, large droppings are from a large bear. Bear droppings are tubular in shape when firm and will measure between $1^{3}/_{8}$ and

$1^1/_2$ inches in diameter when coming from an average size black bear. If a pile is found that measures $1^3/_4$ inches or larger in diameter, it probably was deposited by the kind of bear we are all looking for—a real monster. As you develop into a radical bear hunter and have studied droppings over a long period of time, you will be able to determine what larger-than-average droppings look like without having to measure them. By the way, bear droppings are also beneficial to our land, as they actually fertilize seeds of the plants the bear has eaten and provide valuable humus that enriches the soil.

FEEDING SIGNS

Black bears are not neat eaters. When they are on a feeding frenzy, they will trash small trees by bending them down to eat tender catkins or shoots. Berry bushes may be brutally stripped, and other plants snapped off or uprooted. Bears cause a lot of damage to trees and the like, and this type of destructive behavior is yet another type of sign to look for.

In their search for honey, bees, ants, and other insects, bears will roll over rocks and shred stumps and fallen logs. Learning how to read these indicators can help you determine when the hungry fellow has visited an area. Look at the rocks in an area first. If the rocks have been rolled over or displaced, check both the exposed area and the condition of the vegetation under the rock's new location. If the grasses under the rock have begun to yellow and die, it has been a while since the bear overturned the rock.

You can also look for age indicators when checking stumps or logs that show signs of a bear's fierce claw marks. The coloration of the wood and presence of sawdust can tell you a lot about when the stump or log was ravaged. If loose sawdust is still there, you can be reasonably sure the damage was recent, at least since the last good rain. If no sawdust is found but the exposed wood is yellow or brown, the slashing was done in the past year. Gray wood indicates much more age. An anthill that has been all scooped out is another sign that a black bear is in the area.

The black bear will also strip the bark off trees to get at the soft layer underneath. The hunter may find teeth marks in addition to the gouges left by claws. The same coloration rules apply for aging the claw marks on a tree. Gray means the damage is old; some trees will even grow new bark over the claw marks, leaving grayish scabs the following year.

Early fall is the best time of the year to start checking mast and fruit trees for signs of a black bear's feeding activity. Limbs that have been recently broken should still have green leaves attached. If it's been longer, the leaves will start to turn brown and die. A feeding bear pulling down the branches of a beech or oak tree and breaking them to obtain the beechnuts and acorns creates what is called a bear nest in the Northeast. An apple tree can also sustain severe damage to its branches from a bear climbing all around it trying to strip the fruit. If these trees still have a good food supply, the hunter can almost bet the bear will return soon. Such a location should be checked again next year, and if it maintains a good supply of fruit and nuts, the bear most likely will return there to feed.

A farm, especially one growing corn, is a natural attraction for a black bear. Once the corn gets milky, it's like sticking a candy bar under a kid's nose; the bears can't resist it. If you can find a good size cornfield located near thick cover or a swamp, you can be assured that the field will have several bears feeding within its boundaries. The best places to set up an ambush would be where you find the heaviest amounts of droppings. Most bears spend considerable amounts of time in thick woodland cover, swamps, and wet lowlands. If you can locate a prime feed source close to this type of cover, you will have a real hotspot. Look for trails that exit the thick cover and stay low to the ground where most bear openings will be.

The black bear will also kill animals and eat carrion. Usually it will devour the intestines first, but it will eat whatever it finds. A great part of a bear's daily activities involves eating, and whether or not he is eating blueberries, thrashing about in a cornfield, or attacking a deer fawn, he will fiercely defend his food source.

BEAR-SCRATCH TREES

Besides climbing them, the black bear often will use trees as a rubbing post to mark his territory. While there are several theories why bears mark trees, I believe mature bears do it as a way of communicating and avoiding conflict. Most bear-scratching activity occurs before and during the breeding season in the months of May through July, so the scratching conveys a bear's sex, status, and identity as well as indicates a challenge to rivals. A boar may also scratch trees to attract a sow during the breeding season. When the scratching posts are close to a prime feeding area, the bear is using it to assert his control over that feeding area.

By standing on his hind legs with his back up against the tree, the bear will scratch and rub himself on the tree to deposit his long winter hair in the cracks and bark while he reaches his head around to bite the tree. Bears also will straddle the tree and lick, rub, bite, and claw it to mark their scent. The height of any bite marks on a tree generally provide a good indicator of the height of the bear. I have seen established bear-scratch trees with long hairs heavily embedded in the cracks reveal evidence of years of rubbing, biting, and scratching by bears.

A bear-scratch tree next to a trapper's cabin in northern Canada.

This bear is taking a break and sitting next to his scratch tree.

This monster bruin was harvested by the author over bait with a handmade recurve bow. The author read the sign in the area to determine the best ambush spot.

BEDS AND OTHER BEAR SIGN

A bear's bedding areas are difficult to locate, because they must be in an area where the bear feels secure. Remember that bears like to bed down in a thick, dense, dark, and cool spot. Look for soft depressions made in the ground at the base of large trees or outcroppings of rocks. Bear hair usually can be found on the ground in a bear's bed. These beds are similar in size to a white-tailed deer's, but the bear's beds are more rounded and circular in shape.

Black bears will make their winter dens in hollow logs, under fallen trees, and in natural caves. These dens have a distinct and powerful odor that lingers in the air long after the bear has departed the area, so try using you nose to locate a den site.

If you thought a bear's track was the only bear sign to look for, I hope this chapter made you realize that being aware of the different kinds of bear sign and how to interpret them can give you the tools you need to determine if the bears you want are supported by a given area. To harvest a bear, you must hunt where the bears are. Preseason scouting can provide valuable insight into the habitat of one of the most challenging trophies to be taken with any weapon.

CHAPTER 4

Reading a Bear's Body Language

One of the most important abilities of the radical bear hunter is to be able to read a bear like a book. If you know what the bear is going to do before he does it, you will enhance your chances to get the optimal shot. Through years of observing wild black bears, this radical bear hunter finally understands enough of their body language that they are not as totally unpredictable as I had once found them. Bears are wild animals, not cuddly teddy bears, and they should be given that respect. But the more you observe them, the more you will be able to distinguish certain behaviors and understand them better.

UNDERSTANDING BODY LANGUAGE

The first thing that a radical bear hunter must understand is that black bears are solitary animals. On very few occasions will they actually spend time around other bears. If it happens, it usually occurs in areas where there is a large quantity of food, such as a bait station, a dump site, a river or stream where fish are spawning, or an area with a small concentrated food source such as a wild berry patch. In addition, a sow will nurture her cubs for their first year, and during the spring breeding season bears, of course, will make contact with other bears. There may occasionally be other times, but they are rare in the bears' world.

Black bears have developed a complex set of signals using their body language. These signs and signals are used to communicate with other bears and creatures in their world. Because they don't have a long tail like a dog or cat, they don't use that to communicate, and their normally long fur makes them unable to use their bulky body to communicate either. Instead, through common sense and survival tactics, they have developed all of their body language communication by using their head, mouth, and neck.

Two mature bears establishing dominance over a bait. CUDDEBACK DIGITAL

When a black bear is in close proximity to another bear, the outcome of that encounter usually is determined by the bears' social status. Mature adult boars are always the most dominant, followed by sows with cubs, then mature sows without cubs, and finally immature bears at the bottom of the pecking order. Most confrontations are resolved by the use of a facial expression, an aggressive stance, a growl leading to a bluff-charge, or running full speed and stopping just short of the other creature. What they are telling the other bear is "I'm the biggest bad-ass in the area, and if you mess with me, I will hurt you." Most times this bluff is quite enough for the less dominant animal to retreat quickly from the area or scamper up a nearby tree.

On a number of occasions, I have witnessed immature bears simply hear or smell something while they are feeding in an area and literally boogie out of there before they even see another bear, because they did not want any altercation. Occasionally if the bears are close in their social status, a serious fight results. For the most part, however, bears will avoid a real kick-butt fight. Black bears are strong and powerful animals, and they could easily inflict serious injury on each other in an exchange. I have witnessed a few of these fights at bait stations through the years, and believe me, the battle is fast and furious with one or both bears taking their leave with battle scars. Once I witnessed a bear bleeding so profusely from a fight that he literally had to drag himself out of the area. It was actually frightening to watch because it makes you realize just how powerful an animal a bear can be if it wants to assert its aggression. It is worth repeating that bears are not the cuddly teddy bears we all hugged as children. They are very powerful wild animals that can inflict serious harm to any human if they so desire. They are indeed a predator, and their existence relies upon their ability to kill other animals.

READING BLACK BEAR BODY LANGUAGE

I have learned a lot about how black bears communicate with their body language by observing them at bait stations and concentrated feed areas over the years. The radical bear hunter will use this knowledge to his advantage while hunting.

A hunter perched in a position to observe a bear's behavior while waiting for an opportunity at a big bear has a definite advantage. For starters, the body language of a bear entering or exiting the area will give you a good indication as to its size. I use the smaller bears as sentinels and sheer entertainment at any locations where a bigger bear may come along.

Let's say a hunter is sitting in a treestand over a bait station and a bear comes into the area. The bear is acting nervous and jumpy; at any little sound it hears, it reacts by throwing its head up to listen and to smell the air for the scent of another bear. Many times the bear will even run off a short distance from the area and return if it determines there is no threat. In this situation, the hunter can bet the bear is an immature animal that is low in the pecking order and should not be harvested.

I have seen a mature boar slip in on one of these immature animals and literally chase it up a tree where the bear will remain for hours, if necessary, to avoid conflict with the mature animal. The old boar walked into the area with its head low below its shoulders, an indication of some type of aggressive behavior. He then used a whole range of facial and mouth expressions to intimidate the little guy, including snarling, baring his teeth, rapidly opening and closing his mouth, and drooling saliva. Such body language indicates an aggravated bear.

On another occasion, I witnessed a mature boar coming into a bait. He stood up on his hind legs to get a better view of the bait, and when he smelled an immature bear, he suddenly went back on all fours and started huffing, panting, and popping his jaws as he stared directly with his head lowered and ears laid back at the other bear. He began an aggressive gait toward the other bear, stiff-legged and slapping the ground with his front

This bear was chased up a tree by another more dominant bear at the bait.

pads. The immature bear rocketed out of the area like someone lit his butt on fire with a flame thrower. And from what I could tell by using my digital scouting cameras, he never returned to that area again to feed. Body language alone establishes bears' pecking order without fighting and causing injury.

I recently returned from a bear hunting trip to Golden Eagle Lodge in northern Manitoba. We knew a monster bear was coming to a particular bait station that I was hunting. On my third evening there, I did not hunt the bait because the wind was blowing off the lake across where my back would be and would have taken my scent directly into the bait. Even though I had been using all the proper precautions for human scent elimination, we decided to let the bait rest for the evening and fish for big northern pike instead.

On our way back to camp in our boat, we had to pass close to the bait, and we noticed something swimming across the lake from the direction of the bait station. As we got closer, we realized a bear was actually swimming the lake. When we approached him closely with the boat, we could see he was bleeding from his head and the water around him was red with blood from other body wounds. This bear had been in a bad fight, and it looked as though he was the loser. Even when we went in front of him with the boat so I could take a few pictures, he would not turn. He was headed for shore on the other side and did not want to turn back in the direction he had come because he knew what was back there—a big old boar that almost killed him. Many times older mature boars will literally take over a feed location and push any other bear that enters the area out of it; the mature bear then has the survival advantage of the best foods.

When a mature bear at the top of the social structure enters a feeding area, he shows no hesitation. He will waltz in like he owns the area, and in reality he does because no other bear in its right mind is going to mess with him, particularly after he shows any sign of aggression toward the other bear. Each bear is an individual, and a bear's personal space or zone will vary from animal to animal. If another bear enters that space, the bear responds by relying more on sheer bluffing than anything else. Usually the louder and deeper the sounds from the bear's jaw popping, the larger the bear. Most times an old boar can easily push immature animals out of his space with nothing more than a good loud popping of its jaws or a deep throaty grunt.

As with anything else, practice makes perfect and the more a radical bear hunter can observe black bears in the wild communicating with their body language, the more he will understand it and apply it to his hunting strategy. Such observations will only make him a much better bear hunter in the future.

CHAPTER 5

Baiting the Black Bear

There are two ways to bait a black bear: the optimal way and the way most people do it. A radical bear hunter knows how to maximize the effectiveness of hunting over bait. For example, he won't hunt over first-year bait because he knows that to be successful a bait site must be seasoned. In this chapter, you'll discover where to set up your bait and what to use for bait. You'll learn how to determine what bears, how many bears, and when bears are working the baits. You'll find out which season of the year and what actual time during a season are best for obtaining quality or quantity of bears.

After more than thirty-five years spent hunting black bears and harvesting my share of them, I have learned quite a bit about these beautiful ebony creatures. Hunting black bears over bait is the most effective way to harvest bears, especially in areas where thick vegetation prevents other hunting techniques—such as spot and stalk and running with hounds—from working well. According to the figures compiled by all the record-keeping organizations, more trophy black bears are harvested over bait. This technique allows the bear hunter to be selective about the size of the animal and the quality of the hide and to determine the best time to make a good, clean killing shot on the animal with the weapon of choice. It also provides hunting opportunities to hunters with limited mobility, older hunters who may not be able to walk long distances, and handicapped hunters who need to stay in one place. Bringing bears into bait, however, is a controversial issue and one I have discussed with many outfitters and hunters. Most of the outfitters recognize that baiting is a productive way to harvest a black bear quickly and ethically. Many hunters who think nothing of hunting over a wolf-killed caribou or deer will tell you that baiting is not a fair chase hunt. Or they'll take a 500-yard or longer shot at a moving bear and believe that is ethical. I think bait hunting is fairer to the animal than those methods because it usually produces good one-shot, clean kills.

Hunting bears over bait has become increasingly popular, but don't confuse popularity and effectiveness with ease. What makes bear hunting so incredibly exciting is the knowledge of the black bear's power and unpredictability. When hunting over bait, that excitement and danger are multiplied exponentially as the hunter must position himself in close range to the bear. This is especially true for the bowhunter. Three factors come into play for a bait hunt to be effective: baiting techniques, hunting time, and stand placement. Each factor is critical, and all play an integral part in a successful bait hunt.

Many hunters think that baiting is easy and that you can just walk into the woods, dump some foul-smelling "bait" on the ground, and bag a bruin. But first and foremost, baits must be well established to become and remain active. This requires daily monitoring, from a distance that will keep as much human scent away from the area as possible. The monitoring is just as important as the bait itself.

Remember that a black bear relies almost entirely upon his sense of smell to detect danger. As in white-tailed deer hunting, the hunter who remains undetected as long as possible greatly increases his chances of getting close to a black bear. Because a black bear uses its nose to find food, it has a much more sensitive sense of smell than a white-tailed deer. Hunters who disregard this fact may never see a bear from their stand, let alone get one in a good shooting position.

A couple of years ago, a buddy and I went on a spring bear hunt in New Brunswick, Canada. In three days of hunting, I saw four bears come into my bait, while my friend did not catch a glimpse of one. It dawned on me that we were doing pretty much the same thing except for one glaring exception: He blithely walked to his stand, directly past his bait in his sneakers, without wearing a Scent-Lok suit. The next day, we dressed him in a pair of rubber trapper boots and one of my Scent-Lok suits, and that evening he had a nice bear visit his bait. Eliminating your scent seems like such a minor thing, but it can mean the difference between success and an unproductive hunt.

SPRING VS. FALL BEAR HUNTS

I believe that spring is the best season to hunt bears for several reasons. First of all, spring bears have the longest and densest fur and the longest claws. Think about this: the bear has been hibernating all winter in the coldest weather of the year. If you didn't get a haircut or cut your fingernails all winter, wouldn't they be long too? Of course they would!

The author posing with an impressive bear harvested on a spring bait hunt in Alberta, Canada. Note the prime condition of the bear's glossy, thick pelt.

Second, in the spring, the hunter is not competing with the natural food sources that are available in the fall, so bears will come to baits on a more consistent basis. Spring is also when the black bear breeding season occurs, so the big boars will be moving around over much larger areas looking for sows in heat. Any sow at the bait will draw in more big boars, especially as the season progresses.

Last but not least, during this time of year, the woods are coming alive. Everything is starting to grow, and the smells of the wild are just unbelievable. It's a great time to be out in the woods experiencing the sights and sounds of nature. In addition, you don't have to share the woods with any other big-game hunters, so your success rates are best during the spring season.

In the fall, especially early in the season, bears will not consistently hit the baits because they have so many natural foods available to them. Additionally, their hides will not be anywhere as thick and dense

Bear taken over a fall bait by author Dick Scorzafava.

as in the early spring and their claws will be worn down from digging and walking around the forest. The later into the fall season the hunter goes, the better are the bears' hides as their bodies are preparing for winter.

It is a proven fact that bait hunters have lower success rates in the fall than in the spring. Just check the record books to see the harvest dates of when the largest animals were taken. The outfitters with the most success during the fall are those who continue to bait a location from spring right into fall to keep the bears coming back to that bait. Bears are heaviest in the fall when they are bulking up on food in preparation for the long winter ahead. From my experience, the outfitters who tell a prospective hunter that fall is the best time to hunt black bears are those who either do not have a spring season where they can offer hunts or they offer bear hunting in combination with another big-game hunt. If fall is the only time you have available to hunt a bear, then go, but I much prefer to hunt bear in the spring.

One big plus for taking a fall hunt, however, is that most of the insects can be avoided. Believe me, bugs can be real pests to hunters in the spring, especially in the eastern portion of North America.

WHERE TO SET UP BAIT

The radical bear hunter soon learns from his experience that all baits do not become active, so it is critical to place the bait in locations where bears are likely to find it and where they will feel comfortable coming back to it time after time.

Start the baits in the spring while the bears are still in their winter dens. That way, they'll find them as soon as they come out of hibernation and start moving around. The mature old boars will be the first to come out, followed by the immature three- and four-year-olds and then the sows with cubs. Setting out the bait early will increase the chances of bears locating the bait site. If legal, start fall baits early in the summer to ensure that they are found by the bears and are continually returned to. Early placement is especially critical in the fall when you will be competing with a plentiful supply of natural food, which will make the bait more difficult to get started and become active.

When deciding on a location for a bait site, the radical bear hunter looks for thick cover near a beaver dam, creek, lake, swamp, or anyplace with water where he knows bears spend most of their time. In the spring, the mouth of a stream or creek where it comes into a lake or pond is a great location, because bears will follow a water system looking for the many different species of fish that will spawn in these streams or creeks. They will also find carcasses of winter-killed animals to feed on in these areas.

One of the radical bear hunter's favorite places to set up new baits is near a bear-scratch tree, because these marking posts are located where the home ranges of two mature bears overlap. Look for trees that bears have marked with their claws or bitten with their teeth. Bears also rub their backs against the tree to deposit body scent and hair on the bark. If you find a bear-scratch tree, you can be sure that two mature bears are in that area.

Another good location for a bait site is along a logging or tote road. The older the road the better, because there you'll find brushy growth along the edges. Bears will chow down on the many different kinds of berries and new growth on young trees found within the roadside vegetation. Abandoned road systems also provide easy walking for the bears. I can't tell you how many times over the years I have spotted bears walking or feeding along these old roads. These locations will prove especially

Black bear skirting a lake in search of dinner.

prolific for fall baits because of the berries that the bears feed on at that time of year. Although places with high bear populations will see bear activity at almost any bait set out, remember that just as it is in real estate, the key to a successful bait site is location, location, location.

HOW TO SET UP A BAIT

Once several locations with good potential for bait have been selected, it's a good idea to set out five-gallon plastic buckets first to ensure that they get hit by a bear before placing out the permanent bait station. This will save time, effort, and the amount of bait you'll need to get started.

The key to starting a bait is not only to bring a bear to the location of the bait quickly, but to have the bear want to come back for more food. For this to be effective, the bear must be able to smell the bait over the longest distance possible. I have tried many different things over the years and have hit upon a combination that seems to work the best all over the North American range of the black bear. My formula offers variety, and let's face it, we never really know what bears will like. Like us, bears want different types of food. Keep in mind, though, that you will need a few items with strong odors to act as an attractant.

Fill the plastic buckets three-quarters full with a mixture of rotten fish, eggs, meat scraps, old pastries, chicken guts, brown sugar, and oats. Pour about a half-gallon of old fryer grease over the top, and put the lid on tightly. Place in a heavy-duty black plastic bag, and set the buckets in a

Getting plastic buckets ready to start baits.

sunny place to get the mixture brewing. After about a week, the plastic buckets will be ready to place out at specific locations. At each site, take the bucket out of the black plastic bag and drill a total of about twenty $1/2$-inch vent holes around the sides and the cover of the bucket. Never drill the holes in the plastic bucket before reaching your bait location, or you will have a smelly mess inside the bag and, if the plastic bag would get a hole in it, inside your vehicle or trailer.

Place the plastic bucket up against a small tree, and secure it tightly with a small steel cable so that a bear cannot drag the bucket into the woods. The bears will not find it easy to open these pails. They will have to bite and claw at the bucket to open it, and any evidence of this effort will indicate that a bear rather than some unwanted critter is hitting your bait. Clear a three-foot circle around the bucket until you've uncovered fresh earth. Then pour about a gallon of fryer grease on the ground over this circle. You can even kick it up a notch or two by pouring a bottle of Wildlife Research Center's Ultimate Bear Lure on the ground over the grease. As the bear is working at the bucket, he will be standing and lying in the grease and possibly leaving a readable track. The grease on his pads and belly will leave a scent trail back to the area for other bears. Every bear and every trip to the new bait will expand the trail of the grease for other bears to follow back to the new bait. This baiting method will be like spreading an attractant scent on the breeze. By leaving their trails on the ground, the blackies lure other bears back to the bait.

For bears to locate your bait, they have to be able to smell it. To increase scent dispersal over a much larger area, try hanging something about six or seven feet off the ground from a tree. A properly used attractant can carry five miles or more on the right wind to a black bear's sensitive nose. Once the bear zeros in on the enticing scent, he will be close enough to smell the brew you placed on the ground for him, and a productive bait is born.

A mixture I like to hang in a tree is what I call bear trail mix. To make it, combine a sack of oats, a bottle of molasses, a two-ounce bottle of oil of anise, several packages of berry-flavored Kool-Aid mix, and five pounds of sugar. Fill a five-gallon plastic bucket with the mixture and a half-gallon of used fryer grease and water, and mix thoroughly. Then fill a burlap sack half full with the concoction, knot the top of the bag, tie a rope below the knot on the bag, and suspend it high enough on a tree to discourage small bears from reaching it. Hang the sack six to seven feet off the ground about twenty feet on either side of the stink bucket you placed on the ground to let the sweet smell carry into the wind currents. The sack is like a piñata at a kids' party. Once a bear swipes at the bag, its

Bear standing up to smell the piñata hanging overhead. CUDDEBACK DIGITAL

contents will spill onto the ground, and the bear will greedily gobble up the sweet, yummy bear trail mix. Believe me, he will remember where he found this great-tasting dessert and will be back for more.

If I can find a beaver carcass, I like to use one at the bait station. Bears love beaver and make them part of their diet throughout almost the entire range of the black bear. If you are fortunate enough to obtain a carcass, tie a rope around it and drag it behind an ATV on paths, old roads, and trails leading to your new bait station. At the bait station, hang the beaver carcass from a tree about twenty feet on the other side of the stink bucket.

As an added bonus to get the bait started, tie a string around a large rag and soak it with Ultimate Bear Lure. After the rag is fully saturated, toss the rope over an overhanging branch approximately ten feet up in the tree. Try to hang it in an open area close to the bait site so that the wind thermals will distribute the smell farther out. The scent of Ultimate Bear Lure is so intense that it will be the first odor a bear approaching from downwind will encounter. It's an intense sweet smell that bears can't resist. Ultimate Bear Lure is kind of like this radical bear hunter's American Express card. I don't leave home without it.

Once you've stocked your potential bait stations, you must check them on a daily basis to determine which ones are being hit by bears. Continue to rebait the ones that have been visited to ensure the bears will

Dragging a beaver carcass behind an ATV deposits scent right up to the bait station.

return. When an area has been hit consistently for a week or so, it is time to establish the permanent bait at that location.

ESTABLISHING PERMANENT BAIT

When establishing permanent bait stations, remember to keep them several miles apart, at least four miles in areas of high bear concentrations and farther apart as the bear populations decrease. Maintaining a large enough distance will ensure the same bears are not hitting more than one of the bait stations.

Several methods exist for setting up a permanent bait station, but I will only discuss the one that has been the most productive for me over the years. I have refined this method many times based on a trial and error and by working with a select group of outfitter friends, including Ross Sawyer and Lyle MacMillan of Grey Owl Outfitters in Manitoba and Duke LaCroix of Raven Outfitters in Alberta. These outfitters have more than two hundred years' experience baiting black bears, and they consistently produce bears at bait stations year in and year out.

The bait that will hold a bear at the bait station should be placed inside a fifty-five-gallon steel drum with a removable cover and a steel ring that can be bolted together to make it secure. Not only will this allow easy access to the drum for replenishing the bait, but the drum can be sealed tightly to keep the bears from removing the cover and easily accessing the foodstuff inside the drum.

To give the bear access to the bait, the barrel will need about an eight-inch hole cut in the center of the drum between the two rings. On the opposite side of the drum from the cut hole, two holes should be drilled just above the second ring on the drum. Make these holes large enough to place a chain or heavy steel cable through them. The cable will secure the drum tightly against a tree so that a bear will not be able to turn the drum on its side or drag it off into thick cover. I have seen a bear move a fifty-five-gallon drum full of bait a couple hundred yards from a bait station into thick dense cover because the drum was not secured properly to a tree. I also have seen bear literally rip the drum from the tree and drag it off into the bush because the drum was not adequately anchored down.

Now imagine this scene occurring while the hunter is sitting in a stand at the bait. Although it may be exciting to watch, what kind of good, clean killing shot would a hunter have at the busy bear? Also, if the bear takes the drum out of shooting range, the hunting day will be lost.

Before placing the drum, look over the area carefully and select a tree that will allow the hunter a good shot from a treestand or ground blind. Try to select a tree about eight to ten inches in diameter around which it will be easier to secure the drum. Run a chain or heavy steel cable

Two mature bears at a bait made from fifty-five-gallon barrels.
CUDDEBACK DIGITAL

through the holes in the drum and tightly secure the drum to the tree with a long bolt and nut. You may need another person to help you get the drum tight enough to the tree so a bear cannot overturn the drum.

Once the drum is secured, remove the lid and place the bait inside. Start with three five-gallon buckets of oats or popcorn, a couple packages of Kool-Aid mix, and a gallon of old fryer grease, and mix with a long stick. Top it off with a five-gallon bucket full of meat scraps before securely bolting or wiring the lid so a bear cannot remove it.

Use a metal rake to remove debris from around the drum and rake out a circle of about three feet of freshened earth. Then pour about a gallon of old fryer grease in this area.

Try to hang a beaver carcass or a pig's head, if beaver is not available, from a tree on either side of the bait drum. Not only will the scent go out with the wind currents and attract bears, but when bears stand up on their hind legs to get at the carcass, they may be positioned properly for you to get a great shot from your stand location.

Once the bait is started, you will want to keep food at the location, so check it on a daily basis, if possible. The time of day you bait is important. I like to bait my stations at the same time each day because the bears get programmed to a disturbance at the location. Placing a hunter on the stand while another person sets out the bait is also an effective strategy. The bears get used to the scent of the person baiting, and the hunter can walk in front of him as he baits the drum and climb into the stand. The result is fewer disturbances at the bait. I have witnessed bears come into a station ten or fifteen minutes after the person baiting leaves the location and drives away.

Once a mature bear has been harvested from a bait location, that station should be shut down for the remainder of the hunting season. If this procedure is followed, the area will not be overharvested and should provide good hunting for many years to come. I have seen what happens when guides take several mature bears from a single location. The area is not able to replenish itself with another mature bear, and in just a few years they are harvesting immature bears.

It takes years to grow big bears, and if you kill most of them in one season it may take years to replace them. Furthermore, if the area continues to be hunted, it may never produce mature bears again. Resisting to kill a bear in hopes that it will mature to a bigger bear is called managing your resources. Image what a thrill it would be for a hunter at a bait to see one monster bear out of every three bears he saw. I'm talking about a bear big enough to stop your heart for a few beats. Good outfitters think this way because they are in it for the long haul. Hunters doing their own

Bear pulling down beaver carcass that was hung at a starter bait.

The outfitter closed this bait after the author harvested the mature boar that was visiting there. JOHN DZIZA

baiting also should be thinking this way, particularly if they want to have their children experience the same type of quality hunting that they have.

FIRST-YEAR BAITS

The first year, bait stations are not as productive as older baits that have been at the same locations for several years. In fact, I do not like to hunt first-year bait unless it is absolutely necessary. It is better to let the bait become established before actually hunting that site. The longer a station exists, the more bears will become programmed to it and the better it will be for hunting. Like a good wine, it becomes better with aging. Bears that become programmed to a location will return to it year in and year out. If they came to a site for food as a cub with their mother, they will continue to come as mature boars of seven or eight years old.

DETERMINING WHAT BEARS ARE HITTING THE BAIT

There are many ways to determine size, color phase, and numbers of bears that are hitting a bait station. The best and most accurate way is to use a scouting camera, a technology I prefer because it tells me what time the bears are visiting the bait station.

These images depict the valuable information that can be captured by using a digital scouting camera. CUDDEBACK DIGITAL

But a hunter also can read the sign a bear leaves behind, whether it's scat, hair, or maybe even a clear print of a track. Remember the larger the diameter of the scat, the bigger the bear. Look for hair left behind from bears working the bait drum, especially around the hole where they reach into the drum. You may also find a clear print of the front paw near the drum in the area that was cleared and covered with fryer grease. All these indicators can help you determine more about the bears, but nothing is as accurate as looking at pictures of the bears hitting the bait.

I like to use digital cameras over 35mm film cameras because I do not have to get the film developed to view the pictures. I simply download the photos to my computer and create a file of the pictures from each bait station. This can be a good reference tool later. I have had great results

Left: **Cuddeback camera mounted on a tree, ready for action.**
Middle: **Bear Safe mounted on a tree with camera installed.**
Right: **Bear Safe mounted on a tree without camera and cover.**
CUDDEBACK DIGITAL

using the Cuddeback digital scouting camera over the last couple of years, but I still use the DeerCam 35mm film models at a few stations. Bear Safe is a great enclosure for the cameras. This completely enclosed metal box, which is laser cut and powder coated, will keep the scouting camera from being bitten and destroyed by a curious bear. And because it can be secured and locked to a tree, theft is deterred.

When setting up a scouting camera, use the bait drum as a reference point. By getting the drum in the frame of the picture, you will have something to judge the size of the bear against. If you set up your scouting camera on one of the trails leading to the bait drum, as I have seen many people do, you may miss a picture of the biggest bear hitting the bait because he uses a different trail to enter the bait area. Also small bears entering the bait location may circle the bait first to ensure that a possessive mature bear is not around to chase it off. Immature bears are very cautious taking their time to enter the bait, and if they smell the plastic from the scouting camera enclosure on the trail, they may try to bite it out of frustration and could destroy the unit, if it is not in a Bear Safe container.

The person doing the baiting should not be the one who sets up the scouting camera. Bears will be used to his scent, and because he may have the odor of bait on his hands and body, he could attract a bear to the scouting camera.

I recall several years ago getting some pictures on my DeerCam scouting camera that were totally black. I thought something was wrong

1. Use a tree to mount the scouting camera. Make sure the camera is not facing into the rising or setting sun.

2. Don't attach the camera to a small tree that will move in the wind. Look for a tree that is a minimum of seven inches in diameter.

3. Clear away any weeds or branches with leaves that may block the lens of the camera.

4. Mount the unit approximately twelve feet on average from the bait barrel, and never beyond forty feet. That way, the hunter will be able to determine the quality of the bears hitting the bait. The top of the unit should be mounted to a tree three and a half feet from ground level. Spray the entire enclosure with Scent Killer, protecting the lens opening with your rubber gloves.

5. Buy a scouting camera with a totally enclosed locking device, such as the Bear Safe from DeerCam and Cuddeback. This prevents a bear from biting the camera and destroying the unit. If the person setting up the camera is not totally scent conscious and allows the bait scent to get on the camera housing, a bear may think there is a treat inside and could destroy the unit trying to get the perceived treat out.

6. Place dry foliage from the area you plan to hunt inside the plastic container with your unit. Do not use wet foliage because the dampness will affect the function of the camera over time. Also try carrying your unit in a Scent-Lok day pack to remove as much of the foreign odors as possible from the unit.

7. When checking the unit, always carry a spare set of batteries and an extra media card or roll of film. You can check the unit while baiting, but be extremely scent conscious so as not to get bait on the unit.

8. Set the camera to a five-minute delay between pictures.

Setting up scouting cameras on trees in strategic locations.

with the unit until upon close examination of the pictures, I realized a bear had lain down in front of the camera to take a nap. I had set up the unit on a tree where the trail opened up to the bait barrel. Because the cover was thick on both sides of the trail, the bear must have felt secure there and decided to nap in front of the lens of the camera.

The most exciting part of using scouting cameras is when you get a picture of a monster bear that you didn't know was in the area. A photo like that can inspire a radical bear hunter to stay more alert and on the stand longer. A scouting camera is a great tool for the bear hunter to add to his bag of tricks and have a lot of fun with all year long.

THE BEST TIME TO HUNT BAITS

Spring—When you can expect bear activity to begin at the bait stations in the spring will vary by location, starting earlier in the south and later in the north, and by weather conditions and amount of daylight. Knowing this information will help you determine when to hunt your own baits or when to plan a trip with an outfitter.

The biggest bears will be out of the den earliest and will be hitting the baits first. As the season progresses, you will see more activity at the baits as the immature bears and then the sows and cubs emerge. Next, expect a short lull in activity for several days when the trees pop buds and the bears feast on the new growth. Finally as the season starts to wind down and the bear rut begins, the big mature boars will be roaming over vast areas in search of sows to breed. The amount of area that these mature bears cover will be determined by the density of the bear population. The larger the population, the smaller the roam area, and as the population decreases, the boars will expand their roaming territory.

Fall—The amount of activity you'll see at baits in the fall will be determined by the availability of natural feed sources in the area. In a year with bumper crops of berries, mast crops, corn, fruit trees, and grain, there will be much less activity at any bait station. You'll have the most success at baits that have been maintained throughout the summer months so that bears are in a habit of stopping by for a free meal. But because the bait has to compete with all the natural feed available in the autumn months, bear activity at fall bait stations is never as consistent as in the spring.

TREESTAND PLACEMENT AND SCENT ELIMINATION

When placing your treestands near a bait location, give careful consideration to the prevailing winds and the wind thermal patterns created by the natural contours of the land. A bear's keen nose is his best defense, and a mature old boar will circle the bait downwind before coming in to eat. Try to find a point of high elevation to place your treestands, especially if the area has hilly terrain. Although not ideal for shooting, placing bait in thick cover will give the bears a sense of security, and they are more likely to visit the bait there than if it is set up in the open.

Place your treestands high enough and with enough back cover in the tree to avoid detection, yet low enough to be reasonable. About fifteen to twenty-five feet depending on the tree is a good guideline to follow. Try to select a bait spot that will allow the most favorable shooting position from a treestand. The distance for a deadly accurate shot is about fifteen to twenty yards for a bow, and twenty-five to seventy-five yards for a rifle or muzzleloader, depending on the cover of the area.

Place the treestand so that the evening sun will be setting behind the stand. Since bear hunting at the bait occurs primarily late in the day, you want to keep the sun out of the hunter's eyes. Evening hunting allows the hunter to arrive at the stand in full daylight and leave in the dark with the aid of a light. Although a hunter can leave the stand in the dark, it is not wise to approach the stand location in the dark hours of the morning. If

Treestand placements at baits are critical. Try to have the stand blend into the tree. JOHN DZIZA

Treestand placements at baits are critical. Try to have the stand blend into the tree. JOHN DZIZA

the hunter has not seen a bear all evening, the chances of crossing one in the woods on the way out is slim. In the morning, however, the hunter runs the risk of encountering a bear on the way in, thus placing himself and his bait site in jeopardy.

Shooting a bear at last light raises a dilemma of retrieving it in the dark. Because the sport of bear hunting can be dangerous, especially for a bowhunter, every precaution should be taken to minimize risks. Chasing a wounded bear around in thick cover in the dark is not a prudent idea. I've done it more than a few times over the years, and it can be pretty hair raising. It makes much sense to wait until daylight to pursue the creature.

Most hunters depend upon blood trails to help them find the animals they have shot. A shot bear will almost always bolt out of sight, leaving the hunter wondering if he made a mortal shot on the bear. When looking for a blood trail, keep in mind that a bear may not give any indication that he's been shot. The fat in a bear's body often plugs up the hole made by the arrow or bullet, and you may see little or no blood, even on a mortally wounded bear.

Scent elimination is crucial
if you want success in
your treestand.

I cannot stress enough the importance of eliminating as much human scent as possible from the hunter. A bear can smell much better than a white-tailed deer, and any hunter who does not pay close attention to this important fact may miss out on getting a bear, especially if it's a wise, old mature boar.

To eliminate scent, always shower and shampoo using quality products, such as those offered by Wildlife Research. Wear a complete Scent-Lok system, including the BaseSlayers head cover and gloves. Be sure to read and follow the manufacturer's instructions for the system's storage and use. Always spray your hands, feet, hair, and face with Scent Killer spray before putting on the Scent-Lok system and entering the woods. Also thoroughly spray all your hunting equipment, including your weapon of choice, with Scent Killer. Once you reach the stand location, spray yourself again with Scent Killer before getting into the treestand.

Several years ago I was on a hunt in Saskatchewan. The outfitter I was with had been trying for three years to kill a really nice bear hitting his bait. Every time he put a hunter into the treestand, the bear would

Wearing a Scent-Lok head cover provides the hunter with an added edge.

never come to the bait until well after the hunter had exited for the evening. I hunted the stand on my first evening, and at the end of shooting light I heard a big boar moving around behind me and in the thick cover behind the bait. I realized that the bear could tell a hunter was in the treestand by either smelling him or seeing his silhouette since the tree had absolutely no back cover.

When the outfitter picked me up that evening, I told him that if he wants to kill this bear he must either move the stand or put up another one in a tree with some back cover so the bear is unable to pick the hunter out in the tree. The next day, while he baited the site, I put up a treestand in a thick pine about fifteen feet from the bait drum. I used a completely reactivated Scent-Lok system, including a head cover and gloves, to ensure that this old bruin would not be able to detect any human odors.

The outfitter gave me a wave and exited the area. It was extremely quiet until just as the sun was setting over the horizon, I heard something behind the bait. It was the old boar. He slowly walked into the bait as if he owned the area. He had no idea I was there waiting in ambush. I watched that old bear almost twenty minutes before he presented a good shot opportunity. When he did, I drew my bow to full draw, anchored, and released my arrow. I heard the loud sound of the hit and watched my arrow fletching burrow into his rib cage before he bolted out of the bait to the thick cover from where he had appeared. I could hear him running

This bear walked right under my treestand but because of my scent elimination efforts and treestand placement was totally unaware of my presence.

More views of the bear fooled by my scent elimination efforts and treestand placement.

through the tag alders as I watched the tops swaying back and forth from the movement. Then suddenly the movement stopped, and I knew he had expired less than thirty yards from the bait. That old boar had a $19^{15}/_{16}$-inch skull and measured 6 feet 7 inches nose to tail.

The moral of this story is that treestand setup and placement and scent elimination can mean the difference between getting your trophy bear and going home empty-handed.

CHAPTER 6

Spot and Stalk

Although not productive everywhere, if you can find a relatively open area with a good bear population, spot and stalk may be conducive to spotting bears and may allow you to have one exciting hunt. If you decide spot and stalk is for you, this chapter will give you numerous tips on where to go and how to do it right.

Spotting and then stalking a black bear is an exhilarating way to hunt a blackie. Moving through the woods on foot to actually infiltrate both its territory and its defenses demands all of a hunter's on-the-move skills. But as you move through the forest, always remember that a black bear is a predator, and you must in most cases be on full alert for any indication of trouble.

Hunting a black bear over bait or tracking one with hounds can provide a great hunting adventure, but actually spotting, stalking, and still-hunting an animal that is perfectly capable of ripping a hunter apart is like no other experience you'll have in the woods. Let's face it, bears have nasty claws and sharp teeth, and they do bite and claw back. How close a hunter can get to a bear for a shot depends on two things: his nerve and skill.

The spot and stalk method of hunting black bears relies on the use of a spotting scope or binoculars from a strategic location. After glassing from a long distance and sighting a good bear, a decision must be made to pursue it. Stalking a bear that is a long distance away and getting close enough to it for a good killing shot is no easy chore, especially for a bowhunter.

If you've never done it before, pursuing a bear using the spot and stalk method can be an exciting new challenge and a very different experience from a typical treestand hunt. Many bears are taken with this method by hunters who are elk or deer hunting and have purchased a

Author Dick Scorzafava harvested this trophy bear on a spot and stalk hunt in British Columbia. JOHN DZIZA

bear tag in the event they bump into one on their hunt. Spotting and stalking usually occurs in breathtakingly scenic countryside; Alaska, the western states, and the Canadian provinces are most conducive to this form of hunting, and no other area in all of North America can compare in sheer beauty. This feast for the eyes alone can be worth the price of a trip.

FIND THE FOOD AND YOU'VE FOUND THE BEARS

Nothing can make a bear hunt more successful than locating a bear. This may sound obvious, but except in a few really incredible places out west, bears are not easy to locate.

When pursuing a black bear, remember this one important fact: The black bear is a large eating machine with a never-ending appetite for food, and its stomach dictates its habits and movements. In the years I've spent hunting and studying these great creatures, I have determined that bears will concentrate on a particular food source at specific times of the

This bear was spotted on a logging road in Massachusetts. He had found and ripped open a bag of trash that was discarded along the road.

year. In the early spring, bears will rush to the first lush green grass along a beach and at low tide will dig in the mud flats for clams and mussels or flip over rocks to eat the crabs underneath. They like to visit alpine grass slides that have been cleared by avalanches in the winter and that sprout rich tender grass in the early spring or open slopes on southwest exposures that green up first. Like a magnet, such areas will draw in bears fresh from their winter den. Along old roads and edges of meadows where bears eat fresh clover and grass, plenty of bear sign can be found.

During the fall when the bears are concerned with building up fat reserves for the upcoming winter, they prefer to eat berries, fruits, and mast crops, although in some agricultural areas, they like crops such as corn (especially when it gets milky) and wheat. In Alaska and the islands and coastal areas of British Columbia, the different runs of salmon, starting with the pinks in June and ending with the silvers in September, contain an endless supply of fatty protein-rich food for any bear.

If you are going on an unguided trip, I recommend contacting the state or provincial bear biologist in the area you plan to hunt to find out what the bears' preferred foods are during the time you plan to hunt. In my home state of Massachusetts, for example, the bears will hit any available skunk cabbage and berries first, followed by fruit, which is mainly apples, before they start eating the corn when it gets milky and finally acorns and beechnuts. Remember that a bear is constantly on the move looking for food within its vast home range. Unlike a white-tailed deer that could feed on the acorns or beechnuts a specific area has to offer for a month, a bear may only feed there for a few days to a week.

WHERE TO GO FOR THE BEST SUCCESS

The black bear is an incredibly elusive animal, and just seeing one in the wild would be a victory in many places in the East where the cover is extremely thick and dense and many of the bears are completely nocturnal. But in locations where the hunter has an unobstructed view and the bear population is extremely high, it is not uncommon for a hunter to encounter ten to fifteen bears in a single day of hunting. Depending on how much a hunter can afford to pay for a bear hunt, the following areas would be my picks for hunts ranging from a reasonable unguided trip to a full-blown expensive guided hunt.

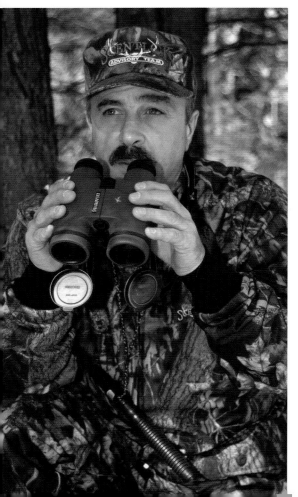

Good optics are critical on any spot and stalk hunt. JOHN DZIZA

Montana—The northwestern portion of Montana around Flathead Lake is surrounded by several mountain ranges, and this area provides plenty of opportunities for an unguided spot and stalk hunt for black bears. With a little research, a hunter should be able to plan an economical hunt, during which he can glass several bears on a daily basis from his vehicle. Getting to within shooting range of one of them could present a problem to the hunter who is not in excellent physical shape.

This area has hundreds of miles of logging roads to drive and glass from for a bear. Keep in mind that many of the roads are closed to vehicle traffic so the hunter may have to hike into those areas on foot. Look for and ask about areas that have been recently clear-cut because they are great places to spot a bear or two feeding on the new growth.

Although this area is not known for producing monster bears, a hunter who works hard and is selective should be able to find a really nice bear. To save on expenses, consider staying at one of the several public campgrounds in the state's national forest. Any hunter on a tight budget who doesn't mind doing it all on his own should seriously look at this area of the Big Sky State.

Contact information: www.fwp.state.mt.us or 406-444-3186

Arizona—When it comes to large record book black bears in many color varieties, this state is a real sleeper. In many areas, more than fifty percent of the bears are color phased. The state offers both spring and fall seasons; the spring tags are issued by a drawing, and the fall tags are available over the counter. The numbers of bears in Arizona has been rising over the last several years, but the bear density is still not extremely high. What the bears lack in density of population, they make up in quality, whether it's a record book bear, large body size, or particular color phase you're seeking.

The best place to start looking for bears is in the scenic and rugged mountain ranges of central and southern Arizona. In the fall, a large majority of the bears move down out of the high country in search of prickly pear fruit. When looking for bears, glass open country and concentrate on prickly pear-laced hillsides. Depending on weather conditions and food availability, the bears may not have moved down into the foothills so you may have to concentrate on the higher elevations. The bears also forage on manzanita berries and acorns, so be sure to glass oak thickets and drainages. If you want to take a spot and stalk fall hunt to this state, I would recommend selecting a quality outfitter that has experience bear hunting the desert mountains in the southcentral portion of Arizona.

Contact information: www.azgfd.com or 602-942-3000

California—The mountains of northern California can produce some nice quality black bears, and the area has received little pressure from other hunters. The top areas of the state for black bear are the areas north, east, and west of the town of Redding in the Shasta, Trinity and Siskiyou National Forest regions. You have to see the landscape in these areas to believe the natural beauty that this area of northern California has to offer. Upon seeing it, most people would not believe they were even in the state of California.

A few quality guides in this area are so confident they can show you a bear that they fully guarantee that you'll see a bear with their no-bear—no-pay policy. Fall is the prime time to hunt this area because the bears will be actively feeding in open areas as they try to build up fat reserves for the upcoming winter.

Contact information: www.dfg.ca.gov or 916-445-0411

Wyoming—The breathtaking Bighorn Mountains of north-central Wyoming just north of the towns of Sheridan and Buffalo have a good bear population. Spot and stalk hunting works quite well in areas that are open enough for a hunter to glass long distances. The overall success rate is not as good as other places out west, but several outfitters who have operated in the area for a long time produce reasonably high success rates on a quality bear.

Contact information: www.gf.state.wy.us or 307-777-4600

Alaska—I have been fortunate to hunt black bears all across the North American continent over the years, and nowhere have I seen the densities of black bears higher than in our forty-ninth state, especially in southeast Alaska and on Prince of Wales Island. These areas consistently produce big bears with large heads and coal black hides that often square 7 feet. Because you can hunt black bears in Alaska without a guide, a hunter is able to set up his own reasonably priced trip. Or a hunter could decide to take one of the many more expensive but good-producing boat-based trips available in southeast Alaska.

The do-it-yourself bear hunter who wants a quality experience should look to Prince of Wales Island. Here, a hunter can arrange a quality bear hunt at an affordable price. This huge island with its diverse habitat, including clear-cuts, rain forests, and open alpine, has black bears almost everywhere. It also has several thousand miles of logging roads that can be used to get around the countryside to glass for a bear. The hunter can take a ferry from the mainland to the island and then rent a vehicle for transportation. Several motels and bed and breakfasts offer reasonable accommodations on the island.

One of my favorite places to hunt for black bears is the coastal area of southeast Alaska. This area ranks near the top for sheer beauty. Every direction you look, you'll find a breathtaking scenic shot like the kind you see in *National Geographic* magazine.

Most of the Alaskan hunts are based from large mother ships that have all the modern comforts of home. The ship will be your mobile home on the water, allowing you to cover a great deal of country in a week. You can glass for bears from the ship or get dropped off on shore for the day to glass from a high spot. All of the ships tow one or more skiffs that are used to get the hunters back and forth from the shore. While on such a trip, it's not uncommon to see a dozen or more bears per day.

Depending on the time of year you go, you may be able to do some fishing for halibut or several species of salmon or go crabbing during slow times. One thing you can count on, the food on these trips is usually delicious and plentiful. It's really like combining three trips in one: a scenic cruise of coastal Alaska, a productive fishing trip, and bear hunting like you have never seen before. Think about taking your significant other along on this trip.

Contact information: www.state.ak.us or 907-465-4190

British Columbia—This western Canadian province has the highest population of bears in all of Canada and is second only to Alaska in all of North America. Although the habitat for bears in BC is exceptional all over the mainland, just off the coast is where I consider to be the best black bear hunting in North America. If you do a search for "black bear honey hole" on the Internet, a picture of Queen Charlotte and Vancouver Islands would appear in front of you. These islands are geographically diverse, ranging from coastal beaches and lush river estuaries at sea level to beautiful and breathtaking river valleys covered in temperate rain forests to the high-mountain alpine where patches of berries flourish. With an abundant food supply and no grizzly bear predation, these islands are a paradise for black bears with superior genetics.

If you want to go on a spot and stalk black bear hunt and harvest a good quality bear, these two islands are the place to go. The bears on these islands are so large that the Safari Club International (SCI) has made a separate category called Island bears for the animals harvested there. When almost a hundred percent of the bears harvested on these two islands made the SCI record book minimum of 18 inches, the new category was added. With the bears' superior genetics and a high bear population per square mile, bear for bear, these islands are unsurpassed by any other place in North America.

No color phase bears can be found on the islands; they are jet black with exceptional hide quality averaging 6 to 7 foot square. The outfitters have done an excellent job of limiting the harvest of the bears to keep the quality high. Most of the hunting occurs from large fishing vessels, which cruise the shores of inlets so that hunters can spot and stalk bears feeding on river estuary grass flats and along the rocky shorelines and beaches. Fresh seafood—including some of my favorites, Dungeness crabs, prawns, oysters, and clams—are caught every day and cooked fresh. Depending on the time of year, you may be able to fish for cod, halibut, and salmon. Because of the quality of the animals and the demand for these hunts, they can be pricey when compared to hunts in other areas in North America.

Contact information: www.gov.bc.ca/fw/wild/synopsis.htm or 250-287-8277

With an innate sense of shyness, black bears will be wary to a certain extent, especially if they have had previous contact with man. They will visually scan for danger, and they can be crafty. For all his bulk, the black bear is a master at remaining invisible. It can keep out of sight until it wishes to make its presence known. This elusiveness, coupled with his keen nose and excellent hearing, make the black bear a difficult animal to hunt.

It follows then that if you choose to stalk and still hunt, your skills will be put to the test. Make every effort to lesson the edge that nature has given this creature for survival. You will need camouflage clothing that blends into the surroundings and Wildlife Research Products Scent Killer and a Scent-Lok Technologies system to eradicate scent. Also take care of noisy clothing and equipment that would give you away during your stalk.

Stalking is not overly difficult. Remember to slow down and take your time. In their eagerness and anticipation, many hunters make all the right moves but do them too hurriedly, and this haste can cost them the chance of taking a bear. Stealth, silence, and above all patience must be exercised when stalking a bear. Calculate all movements beforehand so as to act as quietly and unobtrusively as possible. If a branch snaps or a twig breaks, stop and wait ten to fifteen minutes before resuming your walk, so that any bears in the area will not be able to easily pattern your sounds. Walk softly or in muddy areas that are clear of crackly noisy ground cover, such as dry creek beds or brooks. Don't hesitate to walk through deep mud; it may be squishy, but is much quieter than crunching on dry leaves or twigs. Don't hurry; make every step count as you move closer

Bear spotted from a canoe on a spot and stalk hunt.

and closer to your target. Make your stalk from downwind of the bear; just put your nose into the wind. If you are hunting in steep hilly terrain, always check the prevailing air currents that go up in the morning and down in the afternoon. If possible, use the terrain, including sight-blocking cover such as trees and rocks to disguise your ambush approach. Look for a game trail where the walking will be easier and quieter.

Spot and stalk hunting is more effective in the fall for bowhunters who have to get much closer to a bear than a gun hunter does. In the fall in places such as Alaska and British Columbia, the older mature bears stake out an area along a stream to hunt for spawning fish. The noise of the flowing water and the bear's attention on the fishing will allow a bowhunter to get closer to make a good killing shot without the bear being aware of his presence.

When still-hunting, make sure you use slow, deliberate, quiet movements even when you're stopped. Waiting is the hardest part of a hunt, but you must learn to wait for the bruin to present himself if you want a

This bear was spotted in timber while the author was still-hunting on a game trail.

successful shot. If you don't remain patient, all of your previous work will have been wasted. Waiting is not easy, but it's crucial.

The glossy, thick pelt of the black bear creates a magnificent trophy whether it's mounted on the wall or gracing the floor. Overcoming his natural wariness and his keen sensory systems adds a great degree of satisfaction to the hunt. The awesome power and terrifying potential of this beast can really get a hunter's adrenaline pumping. Spot and stalk hunting a black bear may not be the most productive way to down a black bear when compared with baiting or using dogs, but it is infinitely the most rewarding.

CHAPTER 7

Hunting with Hounds

Hunting with hounds is an extremely viable and exciting way to hunt black bears. When done in remote areas, it can be a rigorous and demanding hunt, but anytime you add the element of dogs, you're in for a rewarding experience. This radical bear hunter loves the action and the music of the hound chase, which when done right, can be like a real-life chase scene.

I grew up following a pack of hounds through the woods of New England, and I quickly learned to appreciate the chop and bawl mouths of the hounds as they chased a bear through the woods to a tree. I truly believe my love of bear hunting with hounds stems from the time spent in the field with my dad and all the stories he told me of past hunts with his family. He came from a large Italian family and had twelve siblings, all of whom quickly learned to be good hunters if they wanted meat to eat.

Nothing compares to the sound of hounds blowing up from a rig as you maneuver your vehicle slowly through a forest road. Here's what a typical hunt with hounds is like. First, the strike dog is released from atop the rig. Once that dog straightens out the track, the other hounds may join him. By the time you have gathered all your gear, the hounds will be completely out of earshot, and the race is on. After following the dogs for hours, you reach the point of thinking you are unable to take another step when you hear the faint sounds of the hounds barking far off in the distance.

Just by listening to the tone of the hounds' bark, a good houndsman can determine if the dogs have a bear treed or running on the ground. Suddenly, a big rush of adrenaline comes into your body, and you take off after them. The excitement builds, as you get closer and closer to the hounds at the tree. When you finally arrive at the tree and look up into its branches, you're amazed to see the size of the monstrous bear up there. That's a true bear race, as we houndsmen call it, and the hounds won that day.

Fewer places today allow bear hunting with hounds, and I believe a time will come when it will disappear forever. If that happens, never again will a hunter hear the mountain music of the hounds echo through a canyon or valley to a tree. Hunting with dogs is a time-honored tradition as old as hunting itself. It would be a shame to see it disappear forever; we must be on the alert for legislation and policies that will preclude this method of bear hunting. If you could trace the ancestry of nearly every dog breed, you would find their partnership with humans goes back to a specific purpose that involved hunting and chasing.

Every year it becomes more difficult to find an outfitter who has quality hounds and who runs them during hunting. This high-energy sport takes lots of time and effort just to maintain the hounds, never mind training them and getting them in shape for the hunting season. Less than ten percent of the black bears harvested across the entire North America range are taken with the aid of hounds even where it is legal to run hounds on bears. Die-hard houndsmen are carved out of a different mold than most other people; having a great running pack of dogs means everything to them. The dogs are their family, and they will devote their entire life to the hounds.

I had a friend who lived in an old school bus in the middle of the woods in the Berkshire Mountains of Massachusetts. The bus had no running water or toilet and just a wood-burning stove for heat. The man was a logger who lived there so he could keep a dozen or so Plott hounds to run bears. This guy was completely devoted to making sure he had a pack of great running dogs, and believe me he had them. Back in those days we had some really great races with his hounds, and we could chase a bear to tree almost all year with little or no restrictions. If it wasn't hunting season, it was training season. After treeing a bear, we would put a telemetry collar on it so the state bear biologist could closely monitor the bear population, especially the mature sows with cubs. Hunting with dogs is an incredible variation of the sport, and one I hope remains an option.

THE HOUNDS

Hounds are bred and trained to hunt bears, and that is what they most love to do. Different varieties of hounds are used to hunt bears, and I have hunted with just about every type over the years. Back when I had hounds, I pretty much ran Plotts because at that time I believed they were the best big-game hounds for bear. Other breeds of hounds, such as Walkers, have done well for other people.

Hounds on the rig.

Mike Kemp with a nice Idaho bear.

Travis Reggear rigging his hounds in an ATV.

Several breeders today have made a real science out of their breeding programs. Mike Kemp from Idaho is one of the country's exceptional breeders producing some of the grittiest bear hounds I have ever had the honor of following. He has been breeding hounds for more than twenty-seven years and in the last five years has developed an incredible strain of hound. The foundation of this strain consists of one-half Trigg foxhound (a running dog), one-quarter Running Walker, and one-quarter Treeing Walker. Mike knows the importance of a good foundation and has had great success in his breeding program by following two basic rules: Breed naturals to naturals, and stay in family lines that are consistent.

His hounds run with a heads-up style. They are the best-handling and fastest-treeing dogs I have seen in my forty years of following hounds. They can strike bears from a long way off and know where the track is right off the rig. I have observed many hounds over the years strike off the rig and go the wrong way for several minutes before straightening out the track, but not Mike's hounds. They will take the track in the right direction most times. When they strike, you better start cutting the other dogs into them, or they will be left out of the race.

Mike told me that after years of working hard to develop this strain, these hounds have finally accomplished his goal. He stated that speed kills. Because they are chasing many a bear that will not tree, the hounds must be able to catch up to the bear, and if they can keep up consistently they can catch anything. The entire pack must be in the race and at the tree. In north-central Idaho where Mike lives, the cover is thick and the mountains are steep. If dogs can handle this terrain, they can run a bear anywhere.

My friend Travis Reggear of Reggear Outfitters has six pups out of the same litter that at fourteen months old are already a great pack of bear hounds. These pups were all raised from a litter he bred, and he socialized them like you would a pack of timber wolves to hunt as a team of one. Any houndsman that followed these young animals from the rig to the tree would never believe they were all from the same litter and only fourteen months old. I saw them tree two bears in four hours one morning. It was thrilling just to watch them work together like a true team. If you love the hounds as I do, you appreciate the thrill of the chase that makes bear hunting with hounds so exhilarating.

WHAT IS A HOUND HUNT LIKE?

Anyone who thinks a hound hunt is easy has no concept of what a true hound hunt is all about, especially one in open country with no roads. So what exactly goes on from the rig to the tree, if the animal decides to climb one? Many big old boars never tree because they have an ornery disposition and just don't have to. Instead they will bay up on the ground and fight off the dogs. I recently returned from an Idaho spring bear hunt with houndsman extraordinaire Travis Reggear. We chased a mean old bear that just would not tree, and after four hours of running Travis's hounds ragged, we decided to pour the coals to him with the addition of hounds from two of Travis's friends, hound breeders Mike Kemp and Mike Stockton. Now this bear had a total of twenty-two dogs chasing him around. You want to talk about hound music echoing through a swamp and canyon. WOW!!! We heard the hounds coming at us several times, and we actually watched the bear cross the road in the canyon in front of our location and head into the thick timber again.

We could tell it was a good size bear, at least 300 pounds, and judging from the size of his head a mature boar. Male bears of that size not only tend to run farther on the ground, but they have the overall size and disposition to attack and actually kill dogs once they are bayed up by the dogs on the ground. The hounds were squalling, and we knew that this bear was going to leave a few of them dead or severely injured if we didn't kill him soon.

A hound that was injured by an angry bear.

Despite all this dog power, the bear still would not tree. Finally my friend had to shoot him on the ground three hours later. This race lasted a little over seven intense hours through some of the most rugged country in north-central Idaho until the dogs finally pushed the bear into our ambush location across a road within shooting range of Travis's muzzle-loader.

In all my years of hunting, I never saw a bear that would not tree with that much dog power barking at him. And no matter how many hounds we poured to him, I don't think that bear would have ever treed. Treeing the bear is always the object of hunting with hounds, but it is not always the result. I believe that the bear, not the hounds pushing him, makes the decision to tree. I also believe that many times the winner of the race comes down to who has the most willpower on that given day— the bear or the pack. In many states such as Wisconsin, for example, which limits the packs to a maximum of six hounds and does not allow the relaying of dogs, what we did in Idaho would have not been allowed. Regulations differ from one area to the other, and hunters must make sure

Rigging down on a logging road.

they are aware of all the hunting regulations in the area they plan to hunt because ignorance is no excuse for breaking the law. Laws change from state to state, and when you are in big woods you may cross state lines without even being aware of it.

There is no better way to start off a crisp, cool morning of hunting than with a truck full of hounds striking from the rig right away. The experienced houndsman will work his truck uphill to take advantage of the morning's natural thermals, which will carry the bear scent down to the dogs. The strike dog on top opens first, and as the scent of the bear gets stronger, the excitement spreads quickly to the rest of the pack. Once the volume, squalls, and chops of the hounds' voices peak, it's time to stop the truck. The strike dog is cut first from the truck to straighten out the track, bawling slowly at first before changing its voice to short squalls and chops as the track gets hotter. The balance of the pack then is cut from the truck with the strike dog out front, and within minutes the race is on and the hounds are completely out of hearing.

Several hours and many miles, both in a vehicle and on foot, later we slowly sneak into the pack of hounds as the dogs jump and howl at the trunk of a large tree. There, about fifteen feet up, hanging on the side of

Getting ready to rig the backcountry with ATVs.

the tree is a shiny coal black bear. He is popping his jaws in an effort to warn off the group. The three-year-old bear is not what we are looking for on this hunt, so we use the opportunity to take some great pictures before placing leashes on the hounds and leading them away from the tree. When we get far enough away for the bear to feel safe, he comes down the tree like a fireman down a pole, hits the ground, and almost instantly disappears into the rising morning sun. As we watch, we relive the entire race and etch it into our memory banks forever.

What makes hunting with hounds so pleasurable is what we call the catch and release factor of the hunt. The hunter can be selective on the quality of animal he would like to harvest and still experience an exciting adventure by just following the hounds to the tree and taking a few pictures. By letting this young bear go, we are creating another opportunity for a bear race again some day with the same animal. Another exhilarating aspect of the hound race is the incredible places the bear will take the hounds and the pursuing hunters in its efforts to elude them. Along with their tremendous heart, bear hounds have a perseverance that makes the hunter want to follow the race to its conclusion. It's not the harvest of a bear that keeps a houndsman going, but rather the die-hard effort the hounds put into each and every race.

Hound treeing hard to keep the bear up.

Every bear race begins somewhere near a road, but rarely does a bear concede to the hounds by treeing in open or gentle terrain. The winding logging and fire roads in bear country are filled with washouts, rickety old wooden bridges, and downed trees, making access difficult. The mountains, thick swamps, and dense evergreen thickets that bears call home are perhaps the only things more treacherous than man-made obstacles. There are no guarantees when a bear race starts because the bear holds all the cards in this game.

To be successful and safe using the hound method of hunting bears, you must have an in-depth knowledge of the terrain along with an understanding of the bears' habitat and preferred foods. If the hounds are properly trained, they will find the bears. The hunter must get the dogs to good starting locations and then find the hounds afterward, all of which requires experience, preparation, and good woodsmanship.

It's worth noting that being chased by hounds has no long-term physical or behavioral effect on bears as most will return to their home areas shortly after the chase has ended, according to studies we have done on telemetry-collared bears in several locations over the years. When we chased bears in Massachusetts and Vermont to put telemetry collars on them, many times the bears would run for hours without ever slowing down. It was like they were running in the Boston Marathon and wanted to win the race. The physical ability of a black bear is enormous by our standards. Many times when the hounds were chasing a young bear we had to cut them off and pick them up because they never stood a chance of catching the bear. I have been a student of bears and the wild places they inhabit since I was a kid, and I learned more about bears following my dogs than I did from any research textbook. In fact, this foundation started my transformation into a radical bear hunter.

CHAPTER 8

Special Hunting Techniques

The radical bear hunter is an innovator, and this chapter will tell you about a variety of techniques—some unique, some off the wall—that will help you bag the trophy bear of a lifetime. If you consider a black bear's spring and fall activities, you'll realize there are several other methods of hunting bears besides the traditional ones of baiting, hounds, and spot and stalk. These tactics include calling, utilizing a bear drive, using attractant scents, hunting natural and agricultural food sources, following caribou herds in areas of high predation by bears, or a combination of the above. All of these tactics, if used properly in the correct location, can and will produce a bear. I have harvested bears using each of these methods over the years and hope to pass the information I learned on to future radical bear hunters. A true radical bear hunter is not content with merely hoping he stumbles onto a bear while elk or deer hunting. He goes out and makes something happen. These techniques will help.

CALLING

Using a call to bring a bear to the hunter can be exciting and at the same time hair-raising and even a bit frightening, especially if the calling is done from the ground. Calling bears is not for the fainthearted, as it will definitely get your adrenaline going. When a bear responds to a hunter using a predator-type call such as a rabbit or fawn in distress, it comes in looking for supper, and the caller quickly can become the hunted. Just knowing this has a way of keeping the hunter alert at all times. I have had a bear charge in and almost run into me when I was calling on the ground with my back up to a tree. I really don't know who was more surprised—the bear or me—but it was a real eye-opener.

Calling from a ground blind with a partner can be an effective technique. JOHN DZIZA

It is usually safer to call with a partner so one can watch the other's back in the event a bear comes in from behind. A partner can also help to share the calling. If the hunter is alone, he should pick a spot where the least likely approach will be from behind and as he calls continually check in that direction.

Calling bears can be exhausting. Unlike calling any other predator such as a coyote or fox, the caller has to use volume and continually call for approximately thirty minutes in the same location. Start off by calling very loudly with aggression, then slowly back off with short intermittent pauses. A bear will not come if the calling does not continue. For this reason, the use of electronic calls has become popular in areas where they are legal. A day of mouth calling can virtually wear out the hunter's lungs. The key is to be patient and give the calling time to work.

A wide variety of calls, including mouth and electronic versions, are available today. Most calls reproduce the sounds of a rabbit or fawn in distress. Others produce the vocalizations of a bear cub, sow, or boar. All will work in the correct situation, and there is no real science to using them, yet understanding why a bear will respond to a call is important for the hunter to succeed. Don't get discouraged if your bear calling doesn't sound perfect; an imperfect call can still produce results. Any loud squally sound in the range of C-sharp is a trigger to the bear's brain to come in and check out the source of the sound.

Instructional cassettes and DVDs are available and can aid the hunter in the many calling techniques. Understanding the vocalization sounds bears make in their daily activities will help the hunter in his quest for a bear. Generally black bears are not vocal animals. A sow with cubs does most of the communication in the bear woods, and many times an old boar will never utter a sound even when waiting. However, the vocalizations bears do make all have a meaning. Let's analyze these vocalizations so future radical bear hunters will thoroughly understand why these sounds are made. The vocabulary of a black bear can be categorized into three levels.

- **Grunt**—The friendly, contented sounds made by a sow or a boar.
- **Blowing and mouth chomping**—The sound created by an explosive release of air from the lungs when the animal is in fear. It includes lip smacking and clicking their teeth together.
- **Miscellaneous vocalizations**—A variety of sounds, including purring, moaning, woofing, and crying. A *purring* bear sounds like a house cat. A cub will make this vocalization when in a comfortable situation, such as nursing on its mother. A bear will *moan* out of fear. You usually hear this sound when a bear gets chased from a bait or up a tree by a dominant boar. A bear will make a *woofing* sound several times before a false or actual charge. The bear hopes the sound will intimidate or frighten away whatever is making it nervous and uncomfortable. Bears will *pop their jaws* together when something invades their space and makes them uncomfortable. I was taking pictures of a large black bear feeding in a salmon stream in Alaska a couple years ago, and as soon as I got too close he started that jaw-popping sound to let me know I was in his feeding space. I immediately backed out, and he calmed down in a few seconds and began feeding again. *Cub bawling* is a distress vocalization made by a cub. It resembles a baby cry and works on the motherly instinct of the sow. Mature boars also will respond to this sound, but their motive will be to kill and eat the cub, especially if they believe it is a male who may be future competition. An aggressive bear will create a pulsing *encroachment call* when it is trying to force another bear out of its space. A sow will use a *crying* vocalization when she is trying to locate a cub that is out of her sight.

Calling bears works equally well in the dense boreal forests of northern Manitoba and Saskatchewan, the arid canyons of Arizona, and every-

This bear was called in by using a mouth rabbit-distress call. JOHN DZIZA

where with a bear population in between. The key to calling is finding a location to set up and call from, and that can differ dramatically from the spring to the fall. Set up where the bear has an easy approach path; the bear must feel comfortable coming in, and it likes soft dirt under the touch senses on his pads. Avoid muddy areas as bears do not like coming into an area through mud; let's face it, neither does the hunter who is stalking an animal. The bear will feel more at ease on dry ground when stalking his prey. Also remember to set up so the wind is in your favor.

During the fall when bears are feeding heavily to build up their fat reserves for the upcoming winter, concentrate your calling around locations with natural food sources. Also try taking advantage of a bear's other senses, such as sight and smell. Use a fawn or rabbit decoy and add some urine from these animals in a location where the bear can easily see and smell his prey. Such tricks will aid the hunter by making his illusion much more realistic to the bear. Research has proven that the more of the five senses that you can turn on in a bear, the longer a bear will stay attracted to an area. The bottom line is that calling is most effective when you also stimulate multiple senses of the bear—sound, smell, sight, taste and touch.

In the spring when bears are just out of the den and not much natural food is available, a hunter can use calling from a bait station to bring in a bear, especially a hesitant old boar that is circling the bait and hanging around just out of range. A rabbit or fawn distress call works well in this situation. A wake-up call such as a raven/crow type can be an effective way to get a bear motivated to head in the direction of the hunter. Few hunters take advantage of this method when calling in a bear. But if you've ever stopped at a dump and heard the squawking of crows or ravens as they scavenge through the garbage, you'll know what I mean. The sound travels far and sends a signal that means "food" to a hungry bear.

Using sow vocalizations during the spring breeding season also can be a productive way to bring in an old boar. Use it at a location where bears are feeding or even at a bait station, since during the breeding season, mature bears will come into bait areas looking for receptive sows.

Calling is most effective once a bear has been glassed or seen from a distance in a natural feed area. Many times it is much more effective than trying to stalk him, especially in open country such as the West. The weather also can play a big factor in calling. Calling is not effective in rainy or windy weather, but on the right day, it can be an especially useful way of bringing a bear to you for an up close and personal encounter.

Eliminating human scent is critical when calling a bear. The hunter should use all the normal precautions of showering and shampooing with Wildlife Research Products, spraying Scent Killer spray on his equipment, including his boots, and wearing a Scent-Lok Technologies total system, including gloves and a head cover. Also wear a camouflage pattern so you will blend into your surroundings. The more invisible you become, the greater your success of calling a bear to you.

The mature, older boars seem to respond better to the calling sounds of a distressed prey animal in the fall and bear vocalizations during the mating season in the spring. These older bears also seem more willing to take chances than a sow or younger male. Maybe because they are the bully of the neighborhood and they know it. Because of this, they often respond to calling with great aggression. Always be alert and watch your back because you don't want to turn around and find a large old boar in your face. Calling is not easy hunting, but with the right attitude and the right homework, you will find it to be an exciting and rewarding technique to employ.

BEAR DRIVES

A black bear primarily moves during the nighttime hours, but if he feels totally undisturbed he will venture out during daylight. Typically bears start moving just before dark, feed during the entire night, and retire to the thickest, nastiest cover they can find to bed down for the day. Beating the bush with a group of hunters can be an effective way to push a bear out of that heavy cover. This method especially works in a bog or swamp that is prime bear habitat but is difficult to hunt using any other method.

A drive for bears should be conducted in the same way that hunters drive out white-tailed deer. The hunters must be in an area known to be inhabited by bears and be familiar with how the bears use the topography of the land in their daily movement patterns. The black bear has predictable movement patterns, and a hunter can use this predictability to put a bear right in front of him.

A drive works like this: A group of hunters will slowly move their way through the thick cover in the hopes of popping a bear out of its bed and into an area where another group will get an opportunity to take a shot. The drivers should also be prepared to shoot as they may have as good a shot opportunity as the people waiting for the bear to come out of hiding. The group of hunters sitting in ambush will place themselves in treestands in specific locations where bears are known to travel and wait for the drivers to bump a bear out of its bed and into them for a shot. A

This bear was pushed into hunters that were sitting in strategic locations on a bear drive.

drive is a group effort involving many individuals who all share in the spoils if one of the group successfully harvests a bear. A drive can also be a fun way to spend time with family and friends in the great outdoors.

USING ATTRACTANT SCENTS

The use of an attractant lure to bring a bear into a specific location for a shot opportunity is an excellent way to hunt black bears, especially in areas where baiting is not legal. Most of these products are legal anywhere that has a bear hunting season. Several effective products are available that when used properly will attract bears from miles away, just as a bait station would. The beauty of using an attractant lure is that you don't have to carry buckets of bait into the area every day.

To obtain consistent success with this technique, you must find locations where a bear is naturally moving and first set up a treestand or ground blind. Next, use the attractant lures in the spot you want the bear to stop for a shot. Over the decades, I've tried just about every commercial bear attractant available, and a few years ago I discovered what has proven to be the best liquid and gel scents for drawing in a bear from miles away. Brad Hering developed Bear Scents LLC while experimenting in his garage with aromas that would attract bears. He simply wanted something that would work for him, but over the last few years he has

This bear was lured in using Ultimate Bear Lure.

A hunter wearing a Scent-Lok suit
to ensure total human scent
elimination. JOHN DZIZA

refined a product that works for many hunters. It comes in about sixteen
different scent aromas; I have had the best results using bacon, big paw,
blueberry, jelly donut, apple, and corn. Bacon is my favorite, and the blueberry, apple, and corn have worked when I was set up close to a natural
food source. I simply set up a treestand in the cover of the woods and
applied the scent on the vegetation where I wanted the bear to stop. The
sprays are simple to apply and are long lasting. I spray the vegetation
heavily on both sides of a trail about three feet off the ground for an area
about six feet long.

Once a bear gets a whiff of this stuff, he is drawn to it like a magnet. I
have used this product on many occasions at established bait locations
and have watched the bear go directly past the bait to the exact area I had
sprayed with the lure. Then I watched as the bear began licking the vegetation where the scent had been applied. As an added bonus, I like to
hang a couple of Quik-Wiks with Ultimate Bear Lure on them on tree
branches about six feet above the ground. This allows the air currents to

Using a mountain bike to get into the backcountry can make your access quick and quiet.

pick up the aroma and carry it a longer distance. Be warned: When using Ultimate Bear Lure in conjunction with Bear Scents, the hunter could be in for some real excitement. I have seen these powerful attractants draw a bear to a location within an hour of being set out.

I hate to keep repeating myself, but it is critical to the hunter's overall success rate to eliminate human scent in the hunting area. I never enter the woods to hunt bear except on a hound hunt without first showering and shampooing with Wildlife Research Products and spraying down my equipment with Scent Killer spray. I also wear a total Scent-Lok Technologies system, which includes gloves and a head cover. No scent is the best scent when a radical bear hunter wants to get up close and personal with big bears.

NATURAL AND AGRICULTURAL FOOD SOURCES

Starting in late August and throughout September and October, bears will gorge themselves on just about anything they can get their lips on as they try to build up fat reserves for the upcoming winter. Fall is a great time to hunt at the feed source, whether it's some type of berry, apples, corn, acorns, or beechnuts. Bears will feed for very long periods of the day totaling about twenty hours before bedding down short distances from the food source for short periods of time. This increased feeding activity certainly makes the bears more accessible to the savvy hunter who is willing to take the time to determine what the bears are feeding on. In the Northeast where I live, I have had great results hunting wild blueberries, abandoned apple orchards, and standing corn once it gets milky, but I know this method will also work anywhere across the North American range of the black bear.

Inspecting the fresh scat of a bear can help a hunter determine exactly what a bear is feeding on. Finding the most appropriate food source will be to the hunter's advantage. A hunter will also have greater success if he knows the lay of the land he will be hunting and where the natural and agricultural food sources are located before the hunting season starts. That way the hunter will not be spending precious hunting time determining where the food sources are located and possibly spooking a bear out of the area in the process.

Once you have examined the scat and determined the type of feed, focus your hunt on the location or locations of that feed as soon as possible. Don't plan to hunt it next week because the bears may switch to a new food source by that time.

When you have determined what and where the bears are feeding, set up a treestand or move in a portable ground blind. The blind is quicker and quieter to set up and would be my first choice. Many times these feed areas do not have a tree to put up a stand in or the tree is not where it should be for the best setup. The ground blind will also hide most of your movements, and if you have to leave the blind to stalk to the animal, you'll be less likely to be spotted by the bear than while climbing out of a treestand. Always carry a good pair of binoculars (I like my Brunton Epochs) to spot the bears feeding at long distances or to scan the edges of timber along the feed source for bear movement.

Hunting natural food sources is an effective technique for the hunter who is willing to put in his time at the correct feed source. It is also legal everywhere that has an open bear hunting season. In reality, it is not much different than hunting over a bait station, but because it has been an established feed source for years, the bears know where to find it.

FOLLOWING CARIBOU HERDS
Most people have never even heard of this method of hunting black bears, but it is particularly productive for a few weeks each spring in areas where caribou cows are calving their young. In these calving grounds, black bears prey on caribou calves. In fact, in several places

across the range of the caribou, such as the Canadian province of Newfoundland, the mortality rate of woodland caribou calves is between sixty and seventy percent. That's a staggering number of calves that fall prey to black bears. In the world of wild animals, nothing operates on fairness. Consider the newly born caribou calf enjoying its new life until a bear picks up its scent, runs it down, and eats it alive. Is that fair? Not at all, but it is nature.

During the two- or three-week period in the spring when the caribou are birthing their calves, the hunter should concentrate his efforts in the actual calving grounds. Go to a high spot and glass for bears trying to make a stalk on a helpless calf. Look carefully on the edges of the timber for the movement of a bear. You may have to move several times during the hunting day as the caribou move. If you use this method, you should be in good physical condition because you may have to move quickly and for long distances to stay with the caribou. Always try to keep as many calves as possible in view, and pay special attention to the newest born as they are easy prey for the bears.

Bears can pick up the smell of newborn calves out of the air from a long distance and will be drawn to the area. Once the hunter has spotted a bear, he must react quickly and plan a shot on the animal while it is in range. Because of the fast response required and the greater distance of shots, this method is primarily for rifle and muzzleloader hunters and is not conducive to bowhunters. By using this method, a hunter can harvest a big old boar at the same time that he does his part in conservation by saving the lives of a few caribou calves.

Being an innovative and radical bear hunter can lead you to success in a bear hunt. Use some or all of these tactics to tilt the scales in your favor.

- Calling to bring the bears to you.
- Using a team to cover large areas and drive the bears to move in the direction of strategically placed hunters.
- Using attractant lures and scents to bring bears to your stand location.
- Taking advantage of natural and agricultural food sources to locate bears.
- Following herds of prey animals, such as caribou, in areas of bear predation.

CHAPTER 9

True Trophy Black Bear

Most bear hunters know that skull measurement is what identifies the trophy bear. This chapter will tell you how to measure your bear's skull to see if it will meet the requirements for record book status. Body weight or hide size are not true trophy indicators since a bear's body weight fluctuates so drastically spring to fall and hides can be stretched up to six inches. The radical bear hunter also considers color phase an indicator of trophy status with the cinnamon, chocolate, blond, and blue or glacier bear and the white Kermode or Spirit Bear among the rarest.

BLACK BEAR SKULL

In reality, what becomes a trophy black bear is a personal decision since each hunter has his own interpretation of a trophy. For those hunters who seek a black beak once in a lifetime, any legally taken bruin is a trophy to inspire personal pride. Some hunters want a big glossy pelt to grace a wall or floor. Still others consider weight, and any bear over 300 pounds, for example, will be a trophy. To the vast majority of hunters, measuring the bear's skull, with specifications put into place by the prestigious Pope and Young Club for bow and arrow hunters, the Boone and Crockett Club and Safari Club International for guns, and the Longhunters Society for muzzleloaders, will determine a trophy.

A black bear's skull is heavy and massive, usually long, wide across the forehead, and with a large jawbone hinge. When combined with the structure of its teeth and jaw, the overall makeup of a black bear skull is carnivorous, with several omnivore modifications.

Bears make the record book based on skull size only. Neither weight nor pad size matter. Bear skulls are scored by measuring the overall length and width with the lower jaw removed and then adding the two measurements together. To ensure that the skull is accurately and fairly

The author harvested this Saskatchewan monster. His skull measured 21⁴/16 inches.

measured, all muscle and tissue must be removed, and the skull must be dried for a period of sixty days, which will result in a slight shrinkage of the skull. How it is cleaned will determine how much shrinkage occurs.

To be hailed a bowhunting trophy and entered into the book for Pope and Young, a bear skull must measure at least 18 inches. To qualify for Boone and Crockett, the skull measurement must be 21 inches for the all-time book and 20 inches for the recording period book. The SCI and Longhunters Society require a bear skull to be 18 inches for entry. A bear that has been bagged with a bow and has a skull measuring 20 or 21 inches can be listed in both Pope and Young and Boone and Crockett. The current world-record black bear had a skull that scored a staggering 23¹⁰/16 inches and was picked up in Sanpete County, Utah, in 1975. This skull has a greatest length without the lower jaw of 14¹²/16 inches and a greatest width of 8¹⁴/16 inches.

Official measurers usually use calipers to get the most accurate measurement. However, the novice or hunter himself can roughly score a skull with good potential by using a tape measure and a couple of wooden blocks. The blocks, which must be longer than the skull, are placed lengthwise along both sides of the skull in a parallel position. The inside measurement between the boards will give the overall width. Moving the blocks to the top and bottom of the skull and repeating the procedure will provide the overall length of the skull. Measurements on bears are taken in sixteenths of an inch, and there are no deductions.

Any damaged skulls are excluded from entry into the record book. Anytime a skull measures close to 18 inches for bowhunters and muzzleloader hunters, or 20 to 21 inches for gun hunters, an official measurement should be made.

SKULL-CLEANING TECHNIQUES

Preparing your skull for measurement is not difficult, but it can be time-consuming, dirty, and smelly. I would suggest alerting your family members before you start any of these methods, so you don't end up in the doghouse.

A bear skull can be cleaned using several techniques, but the following four methods seem to work the best from my experience. If you don't have the time or facilities to do the job, you can also take the skull to a taxidermist and have it cleaned for about one hundred dollars.

1) Simmering technique: This process, known as boiling the meat off of the skull, is probably the most recognized by hunters. Remember that this is called the *simmering* technique, and you should never boil a skull as this will do serious damage to the bones and cause excessive shrinkage to the skull.

First, remove as much meat as possible from the skull with a sharp knife; also cut off the eyeballs, tongue, and any other tissue that can be easily removed with a knife. This will greatly reduce the cleaning process. If you can, completely submerge the skull in a bucket of water for a week or so to soften up the tissue before starting the simmering process.

Next, submerge the skull in a large pot of water, adding sodium carbonate to speed up the simmering process. Now simmer the skull in the pot just as if you were making a batch of soup with meat on large bones. Carefully watch the brew until you see the meat literally start falling off the bone. To avoid boiling the skull, set the stove on a low setting.

Once the meat can be peeled off the skull easily by hand, remove the skull and clean it under running water. Repeat the process as necessary until all the meat and tissue are removed from the skull. Then use a soft wire and or a nylon brush to remove any last bits of tissue clinging to the skull. The brain cavity also should be cleaned out, and at this point in the process it should be very soft and runny, so that it comes out quite easily with a little water pressure. If any brain material remains, you may have to use a hook tool made out of eight-gauge wire to remove it. Flatten the wire with a hammer, and bend it as needed to get into the cavity and remove the remaining tissue material. Be sure to check the skull for any missing teeth at this point before the water from the pot is discarded. If you spot any missing teeth, remove them from the pot and put them in a container so that they can be put back into the skull at a later time.

Place the skull in a safe place in the sun for a few days to dry completely. Once the skull is dry, it is ready to be bleached white. Put the skull in a five-gallon plastic bucket, and submerge it in peroxide, which is available at all beauty supply stores. Cover the bucket with a lid, and leave for approximately twelve hours or until the skull is white. Remove the skull when it turns white, and place it in a sunny place for several days to dry properly. At this point, you can glue any loose or missing teeth back in with 3M's Super Glue, which dries quickly and stays clear. Now the skull is ready to be sprayed with one coat of lacquer sanding sealer, followed by two to three coats of matte-finish polyurethane. This will seal the skull so it will not yellow and will be easy to clean.

2) Maceration technique: Again, use a knife to remove as much of the biggest parts of flesh and tissue as possible. Completely submerge the skull in water inside a five-gallon bucket. Add one-half a box of baking soda to speed up the growth of bacteria. Place the bucket outside in a sunny area, the warmer the temperatures the better. The sun will stimulate the bacteria growth in the bucket of water and start eating away the tissue. Depending on the outside temperatures, this process can take as little as a few weeks to a couple months. The water should be checked every few days, and if the water gets murky and gross with floating meat tissue, it should be partially replaced. Always leave some of the old water in the bucket to keep the bacteria working.

The skull is ready to come out of the bucket when the meat literally falls off the skull and can be easily removed by hand. In most cases, you will not even need a knife to scrape off the meat. Take the skull out of the bucket and rinse it thoroughly with fresh clean water. Then scrub it with a soft nylon brush until it is completely cleaned, making sure the brain tissue is completely out of the cavity. At this point, you can follow the drying, whitening, and finishing processes listed under the simmering technique.

3) Plastic bag technique: This procedure for cleaning the skull works best during the warm temperatures of the hot summer months. Place the

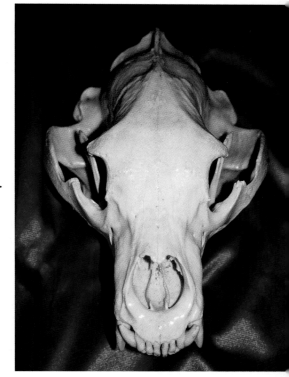

A cleaned and bleached bear skull.

skull in a heavy-gauge plastic bag, removing any big chunks of meat before sealing the bag. Then hang the bag in a tree using a heavy wire or cable so no animals will be able to get at it and pull it down. Let the bag sit in the hot sun for a few weeks during which time the heat inside the bag will encourage the growth of bacteria and insects will find their way into the bag to speed up the decaying process. Be sure to check the skull every couple of days, and without opening the bag, rotate the skull in the bag. Believe me, the smell will be bad enough without opening the bag. Once the meat on the skull has deteriorated enough to literally fall off, remove the skull from the bag. Clean it well under warm water in a sink or with a hose for the pressure, making sure all the brain matter is completely removed. The brain tissue should be soft enough to rinse out easily, but if it isn't, remove it with a wire hook. Then follow the steps mentioned in the simmering technique for drying, whitening, and finishing the skull.

4) Dermestid beetle technique: In my opinion, cleaning a skull using this technique is by far the best method for several reasons: The skull will not shrink as it may with other methods, and no bone damage, especially to the delicate nasal membranes, will occur. No wonder using dermestid beetles is the preferred technique for museums around the world.

Dermestid beetle colonies are available from most taxidermists. Check out their Web sites or contact a taxidermist in your area. Keep in mind that dermestid beetles can be very destructive if they escape from the sealed container into the home, cellar, or garage. They can literally destroy carpets, clothing, wood, or any other organic material. If you decide to use this process to clean the skull, use extreme caution or the money you save by doing it yourself might be spent on replacing carpets or even recapping mounts.

Before placing the skull into a terrarium with the dermestid beetles, remove as much meat and tissue material as possible with a sharp knife. If the flesh is dry on the skull, soak it in water for a couple of hours to make it easier for the beetles to consume the flesh. Then place the skull in the container, and make sure the cover is secure so that the beetles cannot escape. Because the beetles like a moist, dark environment, store the container in a dark area with high humidity. Spray mist the skull with water daily to keep it moist, but be careful not to overspray the skull or mold will start to grow in the enclosure. The total process can take as little as a few days to several weeks, depending on the freshness of the tissue on the skull and the amount of and the appetite of the dermestid beetles used. Many taxidermists will use a couple of containers and move the skull into a new container of beetles if the process slows down.

Once the skull is cleaned by the beetles, remove the skull, rinse it thoroughly under warm water, and use a soft-bristled nylon brush to remove any remaining material. Make sure the brain is completely removed, and use the drying, whitening, and finishing processes reviewed in the simmering technique.

Check with a local taxidermist to find out the fine points of his favorite skull-cleaning methods, or do an Internet search to find the names of taxidermists who specialize in this process.

WEIGHT OF THE BLACK BEAR

The weight of a black bear or any bear species has never been used to indicate trophy size, largely because of the fluctuations in a bear's weight depending upon the season. In the fall, in preparation for the winter hibernation, a bear may have increased his weight by 100 pounds or more. A 300-pound bear in the spring is actually a big bear, while a 300-pound bear in the fall is a fat bear. Available food and habitat also help determine the weight on bears in a given area. Bears in Pennsylvania, North Carolina, and Alaska, where food is readily available, usually weigh more than average.

This exceptional spring bear, weighing 460 pounds, was harvested at a fly-in lake area in northern Alberta, Canada.

Many outfitters never weigh a bear unless their fish and wildlife agency requires it. Most of the time, outfitters and hunters alike will over-estimate the weight of a bear, especially if it is on the smaller side. An old guide told me years ago that the farther you got a black bear away from a scale, the more it would weigh, and that is a very true statement.

A bear in the northern extremities of the species' range will den longer and lose from fifteen to forty percent of its pre-denning weight. In the South where denning time is shorter, bears will lose less weight. The denning cycle allows the black bear to overcome the lack of food sources that occurs in winter weather, especially in the North. On an average, a bear with a pre-denning weight of 400 pounds will have dropped to 300 pounds upon emerging from the den in the spring. Same bear but 100 pounds lighter. If I could only figure out how we could lose weight like that, I'd be a millionaire.

When the days begin to grow longer and increasing temperatures cause the snow to melt, the bears will start to come out of their dens. This usually occurs during the months of March, April, and May, depending on the year and how far north they are denning. A number of factors, includ-ing a bear's age, sex, fat reserves, and reproductive status, amount of daylight hours, and the food availability in the area will determine why and when a bear will leave its den in the spring. The old boars typically leave their dens first, and sows with new cubs will emerge last. Most of the bears will spend a week or so in the general area of their den, although a sow with new cubs will spend much more time there before moving on.

The bottom line is that because so many factors will determine how much a black bear weighs, a bear's weight is not used as an indicator of trophy size for record book entry.

HIDE SIZE OF THE BLACK BEAR

During my more than 30 years of experience guiding and hunting black bear all over North America, I have found that most hunters rank the quality and size of a bear's hide above its skull size. Let's face it, for the average bear hunter a 6- to 7-foot bear rug on the floor or wall is much more impressive than a 20-inch skull sitting on a shelf somewhere. The overall quality of the bear hide is determined by the length and thickness of its hair, its color phase, the length of its claws, and the hide's overall size. I cannot honestly remember ever seeing a hunter shoot a bear that had rubs on its hide because it had a big head; a large head was just the frosting on the cake, so to speak, if the bear had a good, long, dense-haired hide.

Guides usually measure bear hides as a square, by taking two measurements: the length from hide nose to tail and the width across the front outstretched paws. By adding these two figures together and dividing by two, you will have the squared measurement of the bear's hide.

Bear hides stretched and tacked to a cabin wall to dry.

Mike Mattly from Knight Rifles harvested this monster bear in Idaho. It measured 6 feet, 6 inches nose to tail.

The problem is how does one measure a squared hide without exaggerating the size of the animal? I have spent many years in the field hunting and studying bears, and I believe this method is grossly misused. There is no doubt in my mind that some hide stretching goes on every year. Also, some guides will measure the hide from the tip of the claws, while others will measure them from the base of the claws, which will result in different widths.

A green bear hide can be stretched every which way to increase the overall size, and I have seen a freshly skinned bear hide stretched over 6 inches in the length and another 6 inches in the width for a total misrepresentation of 12 inches. Also many first-time bear hunters have been led to believe that they must harvest a 7-foot bear or it's too small and not considered a trophy. A black bear that squares seven foot or more is a rare monster, and most hunters should be content with a bear that reaches the 6-foot mark.

The overall quality of the bear's hide will also vary depending on whether it's spring or the fall. A spring bear that has just emerged from the den has the most prime hide and claws. These early spring bears will have the longest, densest, and most full hair, and their claws can be up to $^3/_8$ of an inch longer. Their hide is in prime condition because they have been hibernating in the den during the cold winter months and their thick coats are Mother Nature's way of protecting them against the cold. In contrast, fall bears have claws that have been worn down from walking and digging, and they are at their heaviest weights because they have been loading up on food to increase their fat reserves for the cold winter ahead. Although fall bears are nice trophies, their hides are always best in the spring. However, as the temperatures increase and the longer they are out of the den, many bears will begin to show up with rubs on their hides. When setting up dates for a bear hunting trip, you may want to consider what the time of the year will mean for the quality of a bear's hide.

NOT ALL BLACK BEARS ARE BLACK

Although most black bears are black in color with a brown muzzle, and occasionally even a white patch with a V shape on their chest, they come in several other color varieties. Because not all the black bears walking around are black in color, their name is actually misleading. Early European settlers gave them the name because when they arrived here in North America, they only saw the black color phase of the animal. The black bear actually comes in many color phases, including brown, cinnamon, blond, blue, and even a yellowish-white.

These different color phases of black bears are a sought-after trophy among hunters for very good reason—they make a beautiful rug. The classic black phase also makes a gorgeous rug when the prime hide is so black it will actually shine, but the blond and cinnamon are my personal favorites.

A bear's color phases are similar to those found in the Labrador retriever, which is mostly black in color but also comes in yellow and chocolate. A black Labrador retriever can produce a yellow or chocolate offspring if it carries the correct gene, and this ability is believed to be the same in black bears. There is also evidence to suggest that bears represent natural selection, and coloration is influenced by the type of habitat and vegetation in which they live. In fact, their habitat is believed to be the dominating factor influencing the different color phases of the black bear. A black bear in a densely forested and moister rainforested area is usually black in color. Black bears that live west of the Mississippi River, where the conditions are drier and the landscape is much more open, have different color phases. In regions where the timber is thick and dark, the bears appear more black in color so that they will blend into the shadows of the landscape. A bear's color is believed to be nature's way of

This beautiful cinnamon-phase black bear was shot by Phil Phillips on a trip arranged by the author to film a Wildlife Point Blank episode for the Outdoor Channel.

camouflaging the animals so they blend better into the landscape of the region where they make their home.

Since the color black retains heat much more than any other color, the different color phases of the black bear found in the West are much less susceptible to stress caused by the sun. In the glacial areas of southeastern Alaska, northwestern British Columbia, and the southeast region of the Yukon, the rare bluish-gray glacier bear is found. These glacier bears blend well into the glacial environment where they live and are almost impossible to spot if they are not on the move. However, as interbreeding with the more dominant gene of the black color phase occurs, the small population of these beautiful bears is becoming increasingly rarer over time.

The most unique and rarest of all the color phases of the black bear is the yellowish-white phase found in the bears on a few coastal islands of British Columbia and the adjacent mainland. These bears have pigmented eyes and skin and are not albinos. They are called the Kermode bear after Francis Kermode, an early naturalist from the British Columbia Provincial Museum who spent many hours studying this rare bear. Originally, it was thought that these bears were a different species of bear, until research determined they were just another color phase of the black bear.

The Tsimshian people of the north coast of British Columbia believe that these white bears have supernatural powers and were created by a raven to remind the people how a time long ago the land was covered with glaciers. These rare white bears, which are called Spirit Bear, are wild and elusive and are also completely protected by Canadian law while in the white color phase. Many people in North America are not even aware that this bear exists.

TROPHY VS. RECORD BOOK BEARS

Perhaps a few words on the difference between a trophy and a record book bear are in order. Again, determining whether a bear is a trophy is a personal, subjective, and individualized decision. A bear that weighs 300 pounds, lives in a prime food source habitat, and comes from an area proven to support large bears should be able to grow a skull large enough to meet either the 18- or 20 to 21-inch record book skull requirements. If so, it would qualify as both a record and a trophy. If not, it would still make a fine trophy. To satisfy any hunter, a trophy should be measured by the effort that went into the hunt and the real satisfaction and pleasure a hunter derived from the hunting experience.

Aubrey Gale from Scent-Lok harvested this trophy cinnamon bear, which had a skull of over 19 inches, a 6-foot hide nose to tail, and a weight of 350 pounds, quite a grand slam.

If a hunter is bent on bagging a record book bear, patience and discrimination must embody the hunting strategy. A record size skull will be determined by age, genetics, and nutrition, and a good mix of all three must be present for a bear to reach the exceptional properties needed to grow a head large enough to be a record book entrant. Some bears may have an abundant food source, live years in nonpressured areas, and have a large body size, but their gene pool may not favor large heads. On the other hand, even if a bear has genetics predisposed to grow a large head, this potential will not be realized if he doesn't live long enough or if his diet is sparse or not nutritionally high.

Track, body, and head size are perhaps the best field indicators for record book potential. Any bear that leaves a footprint 5 to 6 inches across is a superior animal that probably weighs in at 300 pounds or more. The odds of him having a skull that would make him eligible for the record book are excellent. Bears with skulls measuring over 19 inches, especially those at 20 inches, are rare and represent exceptional trophies. The serious hunter in search of a record book bear should find out which states or provinces are producing record book animals. Those areas obviously have both the gene pool to support skull size and the nutritional advantages to provide that potential growth.

CHAPTER 10

How to Field Judge a Bear

One of the most common mistakes both inexperienced and experienced bear hunters make is misjudging the size of a black bear. Any live bear can appear larger than it may actually be due to a hunter's excitement or fear and the understandable notion that this is a threatening situation. I call this phenomenon "ground shrinkage." Ground shrinkage can be a disappointing and disheartening experience. This chapter will let you in on my secrets on how to quickly judge a bear afoot so you don't make a critical mistake. Once the hunter squeezes the trigger on the gun or lets an arrow fly on a bear, he has made his decision to kill the animal, and he cannot turn back. Hunting is not a catch-and-release sport.

I remember shooting my first bear many years ago. When I saw him walk into my area, my first thoughts were, "What a monster!" I watched that bear almost twenty minutes before I had a good, clean killing shot opportunity. He never looked small in size to me until I walked over to him dead on the ground. I truly couldn't believe my own eyes. He was only an immature male that tipped the scales at somewhere between 125 and 150 pounds. My excitement tinged with fear and my inexperience with bears led me to believe that this was a giant of a bear. Because a bear is dangerous and has a reputation as a killer, we tend to unconsciously add size to it. As it was my first bear harvest, I'm sure all of those factors came into play.

In contrast, this spring I shot two extraordinary bears, one in Idaho and the other in Manitoba. The Idaho bear measured 6 feet 5 inches nose to tail, had a front pad just 6 inches across, and weighed between 300 and 325 pounds. But the bear from Manitoba was what dreams are made of for a radical bear hunter. It was a real monster, one of the largest animals I have ever seen in the wild. His hide measured 7 feet 8 inches nose to tail. He had a 7-inch front pad and a 9^1/$_2$-inch rear pad. The estimated live

Dick's spring Idaho bear taken with the help of the hounds.

weight of this monster was in the vicinity of 550 to 600 pounds. He was one enormous spring bear that had just left his den and had absolutely no fat on him. His neck measured 33 inches with the hide removed, the waist measurement of a small man. His teeth told that he was over fifteen years old, and to top it off, his skull green scored well over the 21-inch minimum needed for entry in Boone and Crockett. Quite a difference from the first bear of my youth.

In between these bears, I've shot many others and looked over and evaluated virtually hundreds more. I'm proud to say most of those were mature boars six years old and older. In that time I have hunted bears from Newfoundland to Alaska with some of the top bear guides. We have shared our methods of how to tell a little bear from an average bear from a true monster bear.

While in the field, the radical bear hunter can key in on several clues to help him determine the overall quality of the bear he is looking at. The black bear is one of the hardest, if not *the* hardest, big-game animals to field judge for several reasons. Consider that the average big-game hunter has spent very little time hunting black bears and thus has virtually no experience looking at bears in the wild. Many hunters do not see a black bear until they go on their first bear hunt. When that happens, any black bear looks huge, especially after a slow week in bear camp. No wonder first-time bear hunters harvest small animals. Because black bears usually travel alone, unless it's a sow with cubs, a hunter has nothing to compare its size against. Bears do not have horns or antlers on their heads that the hunter could evaluate to determine trophy quality.

I remember many occasions over the years either guiding or helping first-time bear hunters bait or spot and stalk a wounded bear. Most times the bear probably did not go far, but because of low light or incoming darkness, we always took the safe approach by returning the following morning. After walking up to the bear lying on the ground, a hunter's look of amazement and contentment often turned to dissatisfaction and disbelief at the generally small size of the animal. Occasionally, a hunter would blurt out an incredulous statement, such as "That's not my bear; my bear was much bigger than that one." I would have to calm him down and explain that the blood trail from where the bear was shot led to this spot so, believe it or not, this was his bear. To this day, I think a few of them never believed it was truly the bear they shot.

So how can a hunter avoid this mistake and learn to size up a black bear so that he finds one he will be proud to turn into a rug for the den?

BETTER WITH PRACTICE

Let's start with practice makes perfect. The more bears a hunter sees over time, the better he will get at determining a big bear from a small one. The quickest way to gain experience looking at black bears is to watch bear hunting videos and DVDs. Many bear hunting shows can be found on the Outdoor and Men's Channels. Watch them. The more shows and videos you watch the better. This viewing will give you years of experience from your favorite chair as eventually your brain will start to differentiate the striking differences among big old boars, sows, and young bears. You'll start to see that old mature bruins move in a completely different manner than a sow or immature animal. The sows and immature bears don't have that sway in their gait, and they move much quicker than a mature bear.

The more a bear hunter has the images of a big bear etched in his mind, the more likely he will recognize the real thing when he finally sees one on a hunt. A hunter has a number of tricks and specific things to look for to help him decide if a bear is trophy quality, but none of them works all the time. The hunter must learn to use them but never to rely on just one item to make the final decision to take the bear.

FIELD JUDGING FACTORS

The radical bear hunter uses many factors to field judge a black bear. These criteria should be carefully evaluated before deciding that the animal facing you is the big bear you seek. Let's examine each of the aspects individually so you have a better understanding of what to look for in the field and how to determine a big bear from a small bear.

Weight—When evaluating the weight of a bear, you must consider the time of year. A bear's weight is dramatically different in the spring than in the fall. When explaining this factor, I will use average spring weights of bears, but remember that the same bear in the fall of the year will weigh thirty to thirty-five percent more. An animal that tips the scales between 125 and 200 pounds is an average bear in most of the North American range. Anything that weighs 225 pounds or more is above average, and one that reaches over 300 pounds should be considered outstanding. A behemoth bear tops the 400-pound mark on the scales, but there have been a few rare bears over the years that have tipped the scales at more than 800 pounds. In Pennsylvania during the 2005 fall season, a hunter shot a black bear that officially weighed 733 pounds. Hunters habitually harvest several animals over 600 pounds and a few just over 700 pounds each year in Pennsylvania.

The biggest and heaviest black bears are always mature males. I have seen a mature sow occasionally get large enough in weight that a hunter would be proud to tag her, but in general a sow will never get to the enormous size of an old mature bruin. The sows I have seen have never weighed more than 400 pounds. A mature boar has stocky legs and an enormously thick body with a potbelly that almost hangs to the ground. The potbelly is much more defined in the fall when the bears are bulking up on food for the upcoming winter hibernation. An immature bear's belly line is much straighter, making its legs appear a great deal longer.

To clearly see bears well enough to evaluate them, always use the best optics you can afford. I use a pair of Brunton Epoch binoculars. They should have large objective lenses that will gather light in the lowest light periods of a legal hunting day. If using binoculars in the spring, a hunter may be able to see the testicles between the hind legs of a bear to determine if it is a boar. This is not possible in the fall when the boar's testicles are drawn up into the lower abdomen and completely hidden by the bear's long fur. But upon careful examination, the fall hunter should be able to pick out the tuft of penis hair that protrudes forward and slightly down just in front of the rear legs of the male.

Hide measurement—Many people like to use the squared-hide measurement on a bear to determine overall size. To do this, measure the length and width of the bear, add them together, and then divide the total by two. I like to use just the nose-to-tail measurement of the bear in my equation. When I was guiding, my recommendation to hunters was to hold out for a bear that was at least 5¹/₂ feet long nose to tail. A bear that measured over 6 feet is a good bear, and one that measured over 6¹/₂ feet is outstanding. Any that extends over the 7-foot mark is huge and very rare. Sows will rarely if ever measure more than 5¹/₂ feet nose to tail because they are always shorter in overall body length than boars.

Here's a trick for the first-time bear hunter casing a bait station: Lay a tree, about six inches in diameter and cut to exactly six feet in length, on the ground. At the four- and five-foot length marks on the log, wrap orange surveyor's tape around the tree. The tree should be placed in a position where the hunter can easily see the markings as the bear walks by it on the ground. This trick will help the hunter judge the length of the bear as it moves into the bait area.

Height—When a mature older boar is standing on all four feet, its backline will be 33 to 36 inches from the ground. If the hunter is hunting over bait and using a fifty-five-gallon drum to store the goodies for the bears, the drum can be used to help determine the bear's height. Most drums have two rings that the hunter can use to estimate a bear's height. A good rule of thumb is if the backline of the bear is over the second ring on the drum the bear is a good size. If the backline is even or above the top of the drum, the bear is huge. If there is no drum at the site, you could get the same effect by placing surveyor's tape thirty-three inches from the ground on a couple of trees.

Evaluating a bear's head size—A big old boar has a large blocky, triangular-shaped head with ears that appear small in comparison to the overall size of its head. The ears on a bear stop growing at an early age while the skull continues to grow. Usually the bigger the bear, the wider apart the ears will be. A bear with at least 8 inches between the inside tips of the ears will be a record-class animal. The larger the ears appear on the head and the closer together they are usually indicate a smaller bear. The mature older boars will have what appears to be a short muzzle that looks almost square, while the younger immature bears' and sows' muzzles will appear much longer and pointed on a more slanting head.

Track measurement—The hunter can measure across the width of the front pad print of a bear and with a simple formula quite accurately determine the size of the bear. As the old saying goes, big feet, big bear. I have never seen a sow with a wide front pad, and in most cases a sow's print will never measure more than 4¹/₂ inches across. A mature boar will have a front pad measuring 5 inches or more across the width. To

Look carefully and you'll see that this bear is taller than the fifty-five-gallon drum. A very impressive bear, indeed. CUDDEBACK DIGITAL

illustrate our formula, we will use the 5-inch measurement, add 1, and convert the inches to feet. This would give a bear with a 5-inch track an approximate squared-hide size of 6 feet. A 6-foot bear is a good size anywhere in North America. The radical bear hunter who pays close attention to a bear's tracks will have a good idea of the size of the bear that actually made them.

Hide quality—Evaluating the quality of the hide on a bear is important if you plan on having a beautiful bear rug made to display in your home. From my experience, I've found that guides, rather than hunters, are more concerned about the size of the bear's skull. A hunter would much prefer to display a six- or seven-foot rug on the floor than a bear's cleaned skull on a shelf. Even if a bear had a head as big as a peach basket, I never had a hunter want to take that bear if the animal had a big unsightly rub on its hide. For that reason, the hunter must carefully and totally examine the entire bear's hide as best he can before making a decision to take him. The most obvious locations for rubs, especially on a mature boar, are along the back, butt, and hip areas. I once watched a bear stand up on its hind legs and rub his lower back against a small tree. He was moving his butt back and forth so quickly he appeared to be dancing

This front bear track measured 6¹/₂ inches, which is indicative of a trophy-class bear.

to Chubby Checker's "The Twist." If that wasn't hilarious enough to watch, when he walked away from the tree I saw that his butt was so hairless it looked from a distance as if it had been shaved clean. Such obvious rubs will stand out like a duck out of water, but a bear may have less obvious rubs so a hunter must take the time to look the animal up and down to ensure the pelt is one that could be made into a rug.

A quality thick hide with long hair will appear to split apart as the animal moves because it's so dense. The hunter should also look into the armpits of the animal to determine if the delicate guard hairs are gone. I recommend using binoculars to evaluate the entire hide, even if the bear is at close range. It's worth the effort because you don't want to feel disappointment every time you look at your rug.

Multiple bears together—Mature older boars are loners. If you see what appears to be two adult bears together during the spring or early summer months, the larger of the two will be the male and the bears will be together because it's the breeding season. If you spy a couple of small bears with a larger one, you can bet it's a sow with her cubs because mature bruins seem to detest cubs with a passion.

A sow with two cubs. Note the difference in size between the mother and her offspring. CUDDEBACK DIGITAL

A hunter has many factors he can examine to field judge a black bear in the wild, and with time and patience he will have gained the experience to clearly determine what constitutes a trophy-class black bear. Skull measurement is what all the record-keeping organizations use to size a bear, but it is virtually impossible to determine the actual skull size of an animal by using all the above considerations. When field judging a bear, the hunter can bet in most cases that he has a record book animal in front of him when the factors clearly lean to a mature boar. Don't forget that a hunter must add the bear's age into the equation to meet the minimum requirements for record book entry, whether it be Boone and Crockett, Pope and Young, or Safari Club International. A sow is at her maximum size at six years old, but a boar doesn't reach its maximum size until twelve.

Not one of the techniques discussed in this chapter is totally foolproof by itself. A radical bear hunter learns to put several of the factors together and will try to field judge the bear against its surroundings or other bears in order to gather enough information for making the final decision to take the bear or not.

CHAPTER 11

The Well-Equipped
Bear Hunter

W hat does the radical bear hunter have in his equipment arsenal? This chapter discusses what weapons, clothing, tools, and toys will make your bear hunt more fun, comfortable, productive, and radical.

The radical bear hunter has an array of new tools and gadgets, and he does not cut corners when it comes to equipment. Rather than eliminating the sporting aspect of the hunt, the best available equipment enhances the hunt. I have tested and used every one of the products I mention in this chapter in the most extreme conditions possible, and they have never failed me in their performance. When I travel hundreds of miles to a special hot spot in search of a trophy bear, I want to have total confidence in a product and rely on it to perform its function under all conditions.

I am not providing a paid advertisement for any of these products; rather I am trying to help the average hunter sift through all the equipment available by explaining why I use a particular product and how it can help him in future hunts.

WEAPONS AND ACCESSORIES

The most important piece of equipment for a hunter is his bow or firearm. Bows especially have come a long way in the last decade or so. Compound bows today are faster, lighter, more accurate, and more forgiving than ever before. Although hunters still require hours of practice to become proficient in using bows, today's bows allow many more people the opportunity to enjoy the sport of archery hunting.

I shoot with a Mathews, the company that invented the single-cam technology for the compound bow. There are eight advantages of single-cam technology. The bows are more efficient, forgiving, and accurate, have less recoil, vibration, noise, and maintenance, and experience no synchronization problems. Single-cam technology is the foundation upon which Mathews builds every bow. Combine this simple yet revolutionary technology with other Mathews innovations, such as the perimeter-weighted cam, harmonic damping, and parallel limb design, and you'll see why the company lives up to its famous quote in the industry, "Catch Us If You Can." Matthews makes the best all-around bows in the world.

My archery accessories are made by either Mathews or Montana Black Gold. I use the Mathews arrow web quiver in the detachable model because I can easily remove it from my bow with two little wing nuts. The grippers adjust to hold any size arrow shaft. It has its own quiet harmonic dampeners that eat up any vibration, and its machined aluminum construction provides lightweight durability.

Bowsights also have advanced dramatically in the last decade. Fiber optics are especially important to the bear hunter as most of the hunting action occurs in low light conditions, either just after first light or just before dark. The Black Gold Flashpoint is by far the best and brightest bowsight I've ever used. I find it to be invaluable when hunting bears with my Mathews bow.

The arrow rest I prefer is a FreeFall. This cordless fall-away rest eliminates the potential for equipment problems. I prefer a fall-away rest because it forgives any shooter error that may occur. When my adrenaline is pumping in the presence of a big bear, things can and do go wrong. That's why I choose equipment that alleviates this possibility.

With their many desirable features, Carbon Express arrows shoot straight and true every single shot. The arrows have a patented BuffTuff process that delivers unparalleled strength and durability. Not only does BuffTuff produce a durable arrow, but it is one of the safest carbon arrows on the market. BuffTuff provides a quieter draw and easier arrow removal from targets. Its innovative design also makes it a breeze to fletch arrows. The BullDog nock collars, which give arrow shafts unrelenting strength and durability for nock-end impacts, fit seamlessly over the nock end of an arrow.

Each Carbon Express shaft is checked to $1/10,000$ of an inch. The arrow's straightness tolerances are maximum measurements, not averages like with the arrows of most manufacturers. Every arrow is electronically sorted to provide remarkable weight accuracy and consistency within each dozen.

Spine consistency is the number-one factor in arrow performance. Unlike most manufacturers that grind carbon from the shaft to change the wall thickness of the spine, resulting in a weak arrow with inconsistent wall thicknesses, Carbon Express insists on the highest grades of carbon fiber and the same exacting manufacturing process for every shaft. The company's arrows are manufactured using carbon of varying thicknesses to custom build a lighter and stiffer shaft without grinding.

Bohning's revolutionary Blazer broadhead vane has changed the way I think about arrow guidance. Most of us have been led to believe that more is better when it comes to making our vanes or feathers fly like our field tips. The 2-inch Blazer vane proves that theory wrong by outperforming 4- or 5-inch vanes or feathers. How is that possible? Testing has proven that although some spin is necessary for accurate flight, too much can cause your arrow to lose speed rapidly.

What is required is a guidance system that will take over and steer the arrow regardless of what the broadhead is doing. The Blazer with its unique design begins steering and correcting immediately. The combination of the steep leading-edge angle and material stiffness enables the air to flow over the vane in a manner that actually creates lift and leaves the tip of each vane inside undisturbed air. This concept is similar to the drafting principle used in auto racing. The airflow created by the precise leading-edge angle allows the tip of each vane to act like a rudder. This becomes more noticeable when the flatter trajectory Blazer vanes are used at longer distances. The Blazer wrap, the perfect match for the Blazer vane, will dress up your hunting arrows for increased visibility and style. I love to use the orange Tiger Blazer wraps with orange Blazer vanes to hunt bears because they can be seen as they disappear into the ribs of a monster bruin.

The broadhead I shoot is the Rage expandable. It makes a large entry hole, which is critical on bears whose dense fur, thick hides, and fat tend to limit a blood trail. The bigger the entry wound the better, and the blades on Rage expandables deploy from the rear so they are fully deployed upon entry. This also helps with kinetic energy and eliminates deflection. I used to shoot fixed-blade broadheads when bear hunting, but the Rage offers a much better cutting diameter without any of the drawbacks of previous expandables. I shot the biggest bear of my life in 2006 with this archery equipment setup in northern Manitoba and had a complete pass through. The bear went less than thirty yards before it expired.

When it comes to firearms, I like to hunt bears with a muzzleloader. I guess I just prefer to keep my weapons a little on the primitive side. The two key ingredients for a successful bear hunt are shot placement and bullet integrity. All Knight rifles are guaranteed to shoot accurately right out of the box, regardless of the model you select. From the moment you first pick up a Knight muzzleloader, you will know that it's a different breed of muzzle-loading rifle. At Knight Rifles, they understand the importance of tradition and each Knight innovation is firmly rooted in

Author and radical bear hunter
Dick Scorzafava harvested this
bear using his Mathews bow.

hunting tradition, which makes the sport more rewarding for experts and novices alike. Knight continues to offer the most accurate muzzleloaders in the world.

For the most powerful muzzleloader made today, look at the new .52 caliber from Knight. The Long-Range Hunter has the most knock-down power in a muzzleloader. The .52 caliber uses a Powerstem Breech Plug to ignite loose powder in a more efficient manner, resulting in higher velocities. Combine that higher velocity with a big 375-grain all-copper Red Hot bullet, and you have big medicine for those monster bears.

Because of their superior bullet construction, the .50-caliber muzzleloaders will do the trick for a bear at closer ranges of under 200 yards. I shoot and recommend all copper bullets made by Barnes. The 250- and 300-grain Knight Red Hot bullets feature a large hollow-point design, which is great for close shots on bears. These bullets open quickly and create a massive wound channel. The best bullet I use is the Knight PBT (Polymer Boat Tail) bullet, which has the best ballistic coefficients in muzzle-loading. The 250- and 290-grain PBT bullets are the best options for long-range shooting. They maintain better velocity, have less bullet drop, and offer more energy down range than any other bullet on the market.

I also shoot and recommend Hogdon's Triple Seven powder for all hunting situations. My favorite is loose Triple Seven FFg, not pellets.

Dick shot this bruiser with a Knight Vision in 50 caliber.

Loose powder will allow you to vary your loads by 5- to 10-grain increments to get the best accuracy. If you use pellets, you are stuck with either 100- or 150-grain charges and nothing in between. I have also found that the loose Triple Seven powder provides higher velocity than the pellets.

HUMAN SCENT ELIMINATION

If you want to consistently get up close and personal with monster bears, you must eliminate your human scent. Those big old boars have a sense of smell like no other big-game animal in the wild. If they smell you, they will disappear like a ghost. I would never go on a bear hunt without my Scent-Lok clothing; it has made me a more successful hunter.

Here's how it works: As human scent is exposed to the Scent-Lok fabric, it is drawn into the pore structure of the activated carbon. Activated carbon has millions of microscopic pores, cracks, and crevices, which attract the scent particles and create a bond within the carbon. These particles are trapped, while air is allowed to breathe through the fabric. This process is called adsorption. The American College Dictionary uses charcoal in its definition of the word adsorb: to gather on a surface in a condensed layer, as when charcoal adsorbs gases (suck in). Militaries around the world use carbon in chemical warfare suits to protect soldiers. Although these military suits are designed very differently from a Scent-Lok hunting suit, their basic applications are the same. Carbon is also used in multitudes of filtration systems for filtering not only air but liquids as well.

Activated carbon is the most adsorptive substance known to man, and it has been proven time and again to be the most effective system for filtering odors. Scent-Lok, which has been designed specifically for controlling human odor, uses coconut shell carbon, which is more porous and more adsorptive than charcoal for adsorbing human scent.

Scent-Lok products have the capacity to adsorb human odor for approximately forty hours of field use. Once the garments have reached that elapsed time, they can be desorbed in the clothes dryer, and after the temperature reaches 150 degrees for thirty to forty minutes, the capacity to adsorb odors again has been restored.

For optimal scent-free results, in addition to Scent-Lok Technologies products, I have come to rely on the scent elimination power of Wildlife Research Products Scent Killer's total system. When I am using this exclusive, highly complex, scent-fighting formula, bears will walk within twenty feet downwind of me and never be aware of my presence. When properly applied, these two products used together are extremely effective in eliminating my human scent at the molecular level before it forms a gas. No gas, no odor.

George Schrink, vice president of Scent-Lok, with a trophy class Canadian bear.

If you want to consistently get up close and personal with black bears, scent elimination is imperative.

CLOTHING

The clothing that a radical bear hunter wears is another important part of his hunting equipment arsenal. Bear hunting occurs during months with the most volatile, unpredictable weather. You may be hunting in extreme heat with hordes of insects or in frigid temperatures with snow or a hard, heavy, drenching rain. If your clothing doesn't keep you comfortable, more than likely you will move around too much and either risk being noticed by a savvy old boar or lose your hunting day if you're so uncomfortable that you have to leave your stand during hunting hours. If you paid big money for a quality hunt, not having the proper clothing can be a costly but easily avoided mistake.

I prefer clothing made by Gamehide, a clothing line designed by hunters who know what I want and need in a hunting garment. Much of the Gamehide line features a clever sleeve design called the Freedom Sleeve. This simple yet remarkably effective sleeve is attached in an angled position so that when you raise your arms to shoot or climb into a treestand, you won't feel any tugging. This patented feature may sound simple, but I flat out love it.

Gamehide also makes wonderful rain gear. Its camo packs easily yet is feature filled. I wouldn't go hunting in the woods without it.

It may sound crazy, but the only socks I will wear while hunting are made by Thorlo. My feet just feel better in them. Thorlo, which originated the category of "sports-specific" socks in 1980, started with four styles of socks: golf, running, tennis, and basketball. Almost immediately, the company began to receive letters from consumers and doctors relating how its products were solving all sorts of foot, leg, and back problems, such as blisters, calluses, pain, and post-surgical recovery, and allowing them to enjoy activities once again. All I know is that whether I'm sitting in a treestand, chasing hounds through the woods, or stalking a big blackie on a mountainside, my feet feel better wearing my Thorlos.

TREESTANDS

Virtually everybody hunts from a treestand. My preference is a ladder stand. I'm no spring chicken anymore, and although I can still negotiate a climber or hang-on stand, I figure why hassle with it? I hunt so frequently over bait anyway that I usually have the opportunity to create my setup prior to the hunt.

Nobody in the industry makes a better line of ladder stands at a more reasonable price than Rivers Edge. At nineteen feet, they are taller than any of the other stands, but I like to be up where I can get a better view. Rivers Edge makes roomy, feature-filled stands that are extremely sturdy. The company also makes some two-person models, which are great if you want to take along a cameraman or a novice hunter.

GROUND BLINDS

Sometimes, when the terrain isn't conducive for a treestand, I'll bear hunt out of a ground blind. Talk about a thrill. Going eyeball to eyeball with a bear is nothing short of incredibly amazing! Bears are pretty observant animals so either leave the blind out in the woods so they get acclimated to it or brush it in, and make it scent free. The Cadillac of blinds is the well-made, reliable Double Bull, and the Matrix model offers a 360-degree view, which is especially important when hunting bears, which are more apt than white-tailed deer to come in from an unpredictable direction. The silent window system and the fact that they don't move in the wind

Scorzafava blindsided this trophy from a Double Bull blind.

are also vital to a hunter. Once you've been inside a ground blind, you'll find that hunting in a blind is easier than in a treestand. Not only can you move around a bit more, but you'll stay warmer since you're not exposed to the wind or rain.

SCOUTING CAMERAS

After a weapon, I believe the single most important new product for the radical bear hunter to own is a digital scouting camera. Before we had access to these remote cameras, we had to gauge the size of a bear by its tracks or scat or how the bait had been rummaged. Now, with a photograph in hand, we can easily and accurately tell what kind of bears are in the vicinity.

If the scouting cameras that use film revolutionized bear hunting, then the new digital varieties revolutionized it all over again. No longer do we have to wait until we develop the film to see what has hit the bait. Now, we can make on-the-spot decisions as to whether or not we should hunt the bait or a particular area. Simply put a large memory card into your digital camera, and you can have hundreds of images at your fingertips.

Incredible shots caught by a Cuddeback scouting camera. CUDDEBACK DIGITAL

Cuddeback, the leading digital scouting camera, is easily my choice because its technology and performance are way ahead of the curve. The trigger speed, battery life, and flash range—all critical attributes for a scouting camera—are superior on a Cuddeback.

When using a scouting camera, placement of it is important. Make sure you mount the camera so that you'll have a good look at the bear. A black bear is difficult to photograph in the dark or in low light. Make sure you clear any foliage or branches out of the way so the flash doesn't bounce back.

When using your scouting cameras, be aware of scent. Bears are curious, and if you handle your camera after handling bait, odds are the bear will sniff out and pay a visit to your camera. Bears can quickly ruin an expensive camera. To avoid this problem, use clean gloves or wash your hands thoroughly before handing the camera, or best of all put your camera in a protective cage. Cuddeback makes a nifty product called a Bear Safe that is designed to keep a Cuddeback scouting camera safe. A Bear Safe is great insurance for one of your most important hunting tools.

OPTICS

A radical bear hunter should buy the best possible optics he can afford. In terms of overall quality and cost, it is impossible to beat Brunton's binoculars, spotting scopes, and rifle scopes. The quality of these products' components, especially the glass which is the heart of any optic, have given the conventional optics companies something to chase. Constructed for optimum performance and extended durability, these waterproof products offer a variety of extra features, which have taken Brunton to the pinnacle of optical design and engineering. Brunton manufactures some of the most technologically superior, high-end optics ever produced, and what took years to develop will only take seconds to appreciate.

GPS UNITS

Every radical bear hunter must have a quality GPS unit. I can't tell you how many uses I have found for my Brunton Atlas MNS GPS. Its award-winning multinavigation system combined with its popular Atlas functionality make this unit a must have. Brunton has molded ease of use with an innovative blend of extra features and high-speed performance

The right equipment can increase the chances of a successful experience when you're on a bear hunt of a lifetime.

with a dual processor. The StormWatch barometer gives you the current pressure, predicts the next twelve hours of weather, and provides daily trends and a thirty-six hour history. Add an altimeter function and the TrueMagnetic direct access digital compass, and you have a GPS that can truly navigate. The StraightHome feature allows you to find your way back to camp without satellite aid with just a push of a button. Plug and play with all the Atlas accessories, including Info, World, and Topo MMC cards.

TARGETS
Another piece of equipment I take on all my bear hunts is my portable Block target. I use it before I go out on a hunt to take a few shots to limber up. When I return, I use the Block to check my equipment and assure myself that everything is in working order. The Block's layered technology allows me to shoot broadheads, expandables, or field points, and its target is relatively small and lightweight.

CHAPTER 12

Deciding on a Hunt Location

If you want a trophy bear, you have to go where the getting is best. The radical bear hunter learns to play the odds and finds out the best places to go to get a trophy. Some places may be well-known, and others will be off the beaten path. When planning such an adventure, the industrious bear hunter will consider geographic location, seasonal considerations, method of hunt, and color phase of the bear. Before the bear hunter commits to a hunt, he should do his homework and check references thoroughly. A little time spent up front can make the difference between an enjoyable, successful hunt and a "boondoggle." In this chapter, I try to take the guesswork out of where to go, by sharing my years of experience and research in finding a true Bigfoot. I will also reveal places where I have hunted that consistently produce monster bruins and color-phase animals.

If a radical bear hunter truly wants to harvest a trophy bear, he must hunt an area that has the potential to produce these monsters. The more mature bears that an area holds, the better the chances a hunter will find success on the hunt. It actually takes a long time to grow a monster bear, much longer than, say, a trophy white-tailed deer. Because a bear requires more years to mature and develop into one of those brutes we all have dreams of harvesting, I firmly believe that North America has far fewer places remaining where a real trophy black bear can mature than locations where trophy white-tailed deer can be found.

When planning a hunt, the first thing a hunter must consider is where he wants to hunt. Does he want to experience the grandeur of the Rocky Mountains, or would he prefer to hunt close to home? During his bear hunt, does he want to take advantage of other outdoors opportunities such as fishing? I just love spring trips where I can combine fishing with a bear hunt. It's like getting two trips in one. On top of that, the

Dick with a trophy cinnamon bear harvested from a remote tent camp in Alberta, Canada.

spring is a great time to be outdoors as the woods are coming alive, trees are popping leaves, flowers are growing, and many animals and birds are having their young. But perhaps a hunter wants to avoid the unpleasant insect problems that are prevalent during the spring season. If the hunting opportunities are seasonal, the where of the hunt may also influence the when.

In the early spring, the bears have the finest pelts and the longest claws. Many hunters like to hunt in the spring because either they want a better quality bear hide or they want to get out into the woods earlier. For this opportunity, they'll brave the black flies and perhaps even pack a fishing rod to further enhance their trip. Other hunters prefer to hunt in the autumn, when they can escape from the hordes of insects they encounter in the spring. Whether a hunter chooses the spring or the fall for a trip depends upon what the hunter wants to get out of the hunt. He may prefer the fall when seasonal food crops will help him pattern an animal for a spot and stalk hunt, or he may choose the spring for a bait hunt.

When considering where and when to hunt, a hunter must also choose how he wants to hunt. There are three major methods of bear hunting—spot and stalk, hunting over bait, and using hounds in pursuit—and each method has its followers and aficionados. The hunter must decide which method is his personal preference, but since not all methods are legal everywhere, he may have to be flexible if a great hotspot does not allow the method he prefers. This radical bear hunter enjoys all of the methods of hunting black bear, and if an area has great potential for producing big bears, he will be hunting there, using any method that is legal at that location.

Although exciting when successful, spot and stalk hunting offers the lowest probability of success of all the legal methods except in a few locations where the success rate is almost a hundred percent. It's difficult enough to even find bears in the woods, never mind stalk them.

By looking for nut and berry crops, spawning fish runs, or other available foodstuffs in the fall and green grasses in early spring, a hunter can find a location to sit and wait for a bear. The hunter must be cautious if he plans on self-baiting. Not only do many areas have laws regarding baiting, but it can be a costly and frustrating experience for someone without the proper knowledge.

Bear hunting with a guided service over bait or behind a pack of good hounds offers the greatest opportunity for success. Such hunts, however, leave the hunter dependent upon the expertise of the person guiding. To be effective and productive, baits must be set up well in advance. When hunting with dogs, one must still rely on the ability of the guide to find a bear to chase. Many expert and reliable guides and guiding services are available today. A radical bear hunter must do his homework and check references to find one that will serve his needs best.

Any houndsman will tell you that hunting with dogs can be exciting, but just be sure that it is legal. Again, experienced and well-trained hounds will make the hunt more successful so ask for references and check them thoroughly before deciding to go this route. Once the hunter decides what type of hunt and where he wants to hunt, he can plan accordingly.

THE RADICAL BEAR HUNTER'S TOP TEN HOTSPOTS

I've said it before and I will say it again: If you want to kill a big bear, you must go to a location that will tip the odds in your favor. I have hunted all over the North American continent for trophy black bears and have discovered ten locations that consistently produce big bears year in and year out. You will not find a monster bear behind every tree or bush so you must be selective and really evaluate an animal before deciding to take it. The hunter who has the patience to wait for the right bear will usually come home with what he considers to be a trophy. The success rate in the following locations is exceptionally high. They are listed in alphabetical order.

Phil Phillips, a radical bear hunter, harvested this cinnamon monster over bait in Canada.

Alberta

This western Canadian province has an impressive, well-managed population of bears. It also has a very active outfitters' association called APOS (Alberta Professional Outfitters Society), where you can find several high-quality bear guides. I have hunted with a number of them in the areas that will be mentioned. Most of the big bears come out of the northern forested woodlands, but a hunter should not overlook the agricultural areas just north of Edmonton. The province consistently produces bears with about twenty percent color phases, including blond, chocolate, and cinnamon. The spring season is the best time to plan a hunt here, and bait is the preferred and most productive method. This province has many good areas, but I would closely look at the following three locations for big bears.

Along the Peace River just north of the town of Manning is a vast area that produces quality animals with large skulls. Near the town of Fort McMurray in the northeast section of the province are a couple of fly-in fishing lodges that offer spring bear hunts. This area has limited tags and

Remote Alberta tent camps can and do produce trophy bears every year.

habitually produces big bears. The northern pike and walleye fishing can also be spectacular here. Last but not least, the vast wilderness area around Lac la Biche produces some monsters every spring.

For more information, contact:
Alberta Fish and Wildlife
780-944-0313
www.srd.gov.ab.ca/
Alberta Professional Outfitters Society
780-414-0249
www.apos.ab.ca

Alaska

Our forty-ninth state is a black bear hunting paradise. Southeast Alaska, Prince of Wales Island, and Kuiu Island, in particular, consistently produce 7-foot bears with big skulls and thick coal-black hides. If the hunter chooses one of the many boat-based trips available, he also can try fishing and crabbing. The bear species available will be determined by the time of year, either spring or fall, the hunter decides to hunt. I prefer to go in early May because I find it consistently is the best time for big quality bears. Alaskan hunts with a quality operation can be a little pricy, but in most cases you get what you pay for. Few places in North America consistently produce really big bears like Alaska.

The overall number of black bears remains strong throughout the entire forested habitat of the state, and several units allow a three-bear limit. Predominately, you'll find the bears are all black in color within the state, but a rare blue glacial bear is occasionally harvested along the northern coastline. Although a hunter can do it on his own in Alaska, I highly recommend using an outfitter who knows the area; your success rate will be much higher. And if you shop around, you'll find there's not much difference in the bottom-line cost between the guided and the unguided hunts.

For more information, contact:
Alaska Fish and Game
907-465-4190
www.state.ak.us

Arizona

This state has a small population of black bears, but what it lacks in quantity it makes up in quality of animals. Just check the top twenty entries in the Boone and Crockett record book, and you'll find it stacked with Arizona bears. These monster bears can be found in the chaparral, pine, and aspen-fir forested areas throughout the state at elevations ranging from

Arriving in a remote area via float plane is a radical tactic when hunting trophy bears.

4,000 to 10,000 feet. The bulk of the Arizona black bear's diet consists of berries, roots, grass, cactus fruits, insects, and sporadically small animals or a carcass.

The state has a spring season, which is only available through a draw, and a fall season, when licenses can be purchased over the counter. The legal hunting methods are spot and stalk, hounds, and calling. Arizona's black bears have several color phases, including blond, chocolate, and cinnamon, but black is still the prevalent color. Each year, some nice cinnamon-phase bears are also harvested.

Focus your hunts on these three areas of the state where some really nice animals are consistently produced.

East Eagle Creek—This beautiful area is characterized by deep canyons, heavy vegetation, abundant side creeks, and very few open areas. Quite a few trails permit decent access to the area. You'll find plenty of bear sign along the pine tree strings beside the trails and on the bottom of the canyon.

Hannagan Meadow Area—Mixed conifer habitat interspersed with little openings and riparian meadows defines this breathtaking high-elevation area. The bears found here feed on berries along the streams and acorns in oak stands.

Sheep Wash/Cottonwood Canyon—This area may lack accessible trails, but its relatively open space lends itself to a quite easy cross-country trek. Most of the vegetation in this area is the pinyon pine tree, which is from the Pinaceae pine family and is extremely important to the local wildlife in Arizona. Many mammals and birds eat pinyon nuts, which are kidney bean sized and a southwestern delicacy. The area is also covered with juniper and grasslands. The locale lends itself to spot and stalk hunting; hunters should find a high place and use a spotting scope or high-quality binoculars to glass across the area. The San Carlos Indian Reservation is close by, and many large bears travel back and forth between the two areas. Try setting up an ambush for one of those monsters who likes to trek between the two locations. Another promising spot is the White Mountain Apache Reservation, which encompasses vast acreage with elevations of twenty-five hundred to almost twelve thousand feet. Because the area has consistently produced large numbers of quality record book animals, Arizona should not be overlooked if you hope to put a black bear in the record book.

For more information, contact:

Arizona Game and Fish

602-942-3000

www.gf.state.az.us

British Columbia

Although the habitat for black bears is exceptional all over the mainland of British Columbia, Queen Charlotte and Vancouver islands just off the coast consistently produce big bears. These islands offer an abundant food supply, a temperate rain forest climate with a long growing season, and no grizzly bear predation. Among the islands' primeval setting of deep river valleys, old-growth forests, fjords surrounded by breathtaking mountains, and open beaches on the Pacific Ocean, salmon rivers, free of grizzly bears, allow the black bears to feed freely on the spawning salmon in the summer and fall. The remarkable size of the black bears living on these islands has prompted the Safari Club International to create a separate category for record book entry called Island Bears. The average size of a boar taken on these islands is $6^{1}/_{2}$ to 7 feet nose to tail with skulls ranging from 18 to 21 inches. Simply put, if you want to go on just one hunt and come home with a trophy bear, this is the place. Nowhere else in North America will you find the consistency in age and size of bears harvested on these two beautiful islands. Because Queen Charlotte Island receives the least hunting pressure on its bears, I would key in on this island. Vancouver Island has many more outfitting operations to select from, but because the harvests are so well-managed, the island still produces quality animals every year. Both islands are my picks for the best places to spot and stalk a nice blackie.

Spot and stalk hunting only is permitted on the islands, but hound hunting is offered on the mainland. The mainland and islands allow a two-bear limit, and both have a spring and fall season. You'll find a relatively high percentage of cinnamon and chocolate color phases, and even a rare blue-phase glacier bear in a few northern locations along the coast, on the mainland, but the island bears are all coal black. The hunts on the mainland can be made for approximately half the price of the island hunts, but the overall success rate for bagging a quality animal on the islands is almost a hundred percent.

For further information, contact:
British Columbia Fish and Wildlife
250-287-8277
www.gov.bc.ca/fw/wild/synopsis.htm

California

The northern third of this state is home to about thirty-five thousand bears. The mountainous area of northern California produces a few 600-pound bears every season, and the western area receives little pressure from hunters. The Sierra Nevada Mountains on the eastern side of the state provide excellent black bear habitat. The areas just north, east, and west of the town of Redding in the Shasta, Trinity, and Siskiyou National Forest regions are tops in the state for black bear hunting.

Several quality guides in the state actually offer a fully guaranteed bear hunt. They are so confident in the areas they hunt that they have a "no bear, no pay" policy. The prime time to hunt the area is the fall when the bears are actively moving, feeding, and showing themselves in open areas.

You can buy a hunting license over the counter, and spot and stalk and the use of hounds are both legal methods of hunting. Using bait of any kind is not legal anywhere in the state.

For more information, contact:
California Department of Fish and Game
916-445-0411
www.dfg.ca.gov

Idaho

The state of Idaho has a healthy black bear population, which has resulted in an increase in the limit from one to two bears in the northern part of the state. Tags are unlimited, and a license is available at a reduced price to encourage bear harvests in many of the state's wilderness areas. The state

Author Dick Scorzafava with a trophy-class Idaho spring bear.

offers both spring and fall seasons for hunting black bear, and baiting, spot and stalk, and the use of hounds are all legal methods of pursuing a bear. You'll find a high percentage of the cinnamon color-phase bear in a number of areas of the state, especially in the northcentral region.

Follow the footsteps of Lewis and Clark and discover for yourself the beauty and extraordinary diversity in this land of rugged wilderness, which includes Hells Canyon and the Snake, Salmon, Clearwater, and Selway rivers.

The state has several quality guides, and although you can hunt on your own, I don't recommend it because the country is quite rugged and requires lots of good quality equipment to get around the mountains. The success rate with an outfitter is almost if not always a hundred percent, and the state is a great place for a chase with the hounds. The areas to the north and south of the town of Orofino always produce some nice bears over 6 feet nose to tail. The state's road system provides access to vast areas of great bear habitat. In the spring, look for bears feeding in the new green grasses of the North Slope hill slides. In the fall, you'll find bears in high-elevation berry patches that are still producing. Idaho would be my pick for the best hound hunt for a trophy bear.

For more information, contact:
Idaho Fish and Game
208-334-3700
www.fishandgame.idaho.gov
Idaho Tourism
800-VISIT-ID
www.visitidaho.org

Manitoba

Plenty of places offer good baited black bear hunts, but if I had to choose just one it would be Manitoba. This Canadian province manages its resources very well by using a quota system for nonresidents and instituting a one-bear limit annually. Manitoba also produces a large percentage of color-phase bears, mostly cinnamon and chocolate, with a few blonds. The province offers both spring and fall hunts, but hands down spring is the best time to hunt for bear. The exact time within the season will depend on where in the province the hunter plans to hunt. The farther north, the later in the season the hunt should take place. The last week of May and the first week of June are perfect times to go hunting in most areas in the province.

The northern areas around The Pas and Flin Flon receive very little hunting pressure and thus produce some quality trophies. For many years, the Riding and Duck mountains have continually produced some monsters. My favorite secret hotspot is around the little northern mining town of Lynn Lake. This area is in the boreal forest and is almost untouched by hunting pressure. This past spring, I hunted at a fly-in lake north of Lynn Lake. It was basically a fishing camp, and I was one of two bear hunters it hosted this year. Both of us shot monster bears. I liked the place so much that I have planned to return again next year. Such places can continually produce monster bears because the remoteness of the area results in virtually no hunting pressure, which allows bears to grow old. You can bet that many of the bears in places like this have never even seen a human before.

For more information, contact:
Manitoba Wildlife
204-945-7775
www.gov.mb.ca/conservation/wildlife/hunting/index.html
Travel Manitoba
800-665-0045
www.travelmanitoba.com

Two monster bears harvested just north of Lynn Lake, Manitoba, with Grey Owl Outfitters.

North Carolina

North Carolina has more acres devoted to bear sanctuaries than any other state in the lower forty-eight, and this has resulted in an increase in the overall numbers and size of its black bears. The state has basically two different black bear populations, one within the coastal region and the other in the mountains. All of the bears are black in color with no variation. As good as the hunting in the mountain region is, the hunters take bigger and more bears in the coastal region of the state, although only a very small percentage of the coastal black bears harvested annually are from public land. In contrast, well over fifty percent of the bears harvested from the mountain region each year are taken from public land. Hyde County has topped the state's list in recent years for overall number of bears and the biggest and heaviest bears harvested. Beaufort County, also in District 1, has been running a close second in the coastal region.

The number of bear and vehicle collisions in District 1 has been rising each year, which indicates that the bear population is growing. Within the mountain region, the top bear-producing counties are Haywood, McDowell, and Graham. These areas are rugged country with good natural habitat; throughout the entire mountain region, hound hunting is more productive than the spot and stalk method. The spot and stalk and still hunting methods are effective in the coastal region where an abundance of agricultural mix and swamps with ripening blackgum berries attract bears. A few guides in the state offer spot and stalk or hound hunts at a reasonable price, and their success rate for getting hunters a quality animal is very good.

For more information, contact:
North Carolina Wildlife
919-707-0050
http://216.27.49.98

Pennsylvania

This northeastern state has a good population of black bears, thanks to now-retired bear biologist Gary Alt. Alt did a fantastic job of managing and producing heavy bears with big heads over the years, and the state is now reaping the rewards of his work. Bears can be found in almost every county, but they're primarily in the north, south-central, and northeast regions of the Keystone State. Most of the monsters are taken in the Pocono Mountains, but don't overlook other areas. At least thirteen counties have had bears over 500 pounds weighed and officially tagged. Since the state started mandatory registration, six bears tipping the scales at over 800 pounds have been tagged at checking stations. That is as big a bear as you'll find anywhere. The state has no color phases in their bears—they are all black as coal—but heck, I just love a beautiful glossy black rug in front of the fireplace.

Pennsylvania only has a very short season in the late fall, and most of the animals are harvested on bear drives by hunters who know the area. The use of hounds and baiting are illegal. Keep a close eye on this state because there are many more monsters to come out of it in the near future.

For more information, contact:
Pennsylvania Game Commission
717-787-4250
www.pgc.state.pa.us/

Wisconsin

The Badger State has established itself as a trophy hotspot for black bears. Unfortunately, drawing one of the limited quota tags in many units can take a hunter up to nine preference points and several years. For the most part, the bears make their home in a forested region in the northern one-third of the state. The highest density of animals can be found in Zone A1 in the northwest, an area that also has the highest hunter success rate in the state. The radical bear hunter should not overlook Zone C, which is located much farther south, and takes some really good animals each season. This area has some big bears, and the hunting pressure is much less here than in other areas. It is legal to bait, hound hunt, or still hunt for black bears in Wisconsin, but most of the bears are taken over bait and hounds.

For more information, contact:
Wisconsin Department of Natural Resources
608-266-2621
www.dnr.state.wi.us

CHAPTER 13

Picking an Outfitter

The best way to get your bear is to go where the bears are and to find an outfitter who will get the job done for you. Those hunters who think they can thumb through a magazine and pick a guide at random without doing their homework usually will be disappointed. Just the other day, I surfed the web for "black bear hunting guides" and got over two million hits. Wow!! Do you think the hunter seeking to go on a black bear hunt could simply scroll through all those hits and select the perfect match for his hunt? What are the chances he'll find a guide in an exceptional hunting area with many mature old boars that are every color of the rainbow? Doubtful, unless he was extremely lucky or a very fast reader. He probably would have a better chance of winning the state lottery.

Choosing a guide requires some groundwork on the hunter's part. But if he wants to be paired with a competent and experienced guide who can position the hunter for the best opportunity to shoot at a black bear, the effort is worth it. Any hunter who does not take the time to carefully select a guide can end up dissatisfied, disappointed, or worse.

Finding a guide from an advertisement is only the first step in deciding who will lead you on your hunt. It should not be the only way you make your selection. Remember that although most guiding services are reputable and do their best to provide promised services, even the shadiest characters can create an eye-catching ad and pay to have it inserted in any publication in the country. Just because a guide has paid for a quality ad doesn't mean he is the best guide or outfitter for you.

Some guides are just out to make a fast buck and are not in the business for the long haul, so fleecing a few hunters is as good a way as any. Others may be industrious and well-meaning but inexperienced. Still others (the vast minority, I'm sure), may resort to illegal or unethical hunting tactics to bag bears, fill tags, and then quote impressive camp statistics. The old saying "Buyer beware!" is certainly pertinent when it comes to a guided bear hunt.

One of the first things you must decide upon is not which guide, but what kind of bear hunt you want to go on. Guides usually can arrange hunts where the hunter can use any number of methods, including baiting, spot and stalk, and hounds, to harvest a bear. Decide what kind of method you are looking for and where you'd like to hunt and then decide which season is best. After these initial decisions are made, weeding out the guides who don't provide your chosen services should be easy. Once the hunter has narrowed the list to a few guides, the real work must begin.

Write, e-mail, or call the guide. Many times a guide will return your call so be sure to include your telephone number and best times to call in any message you leave. During hunting season, it may be easier for a guide to pick up the phone than jump on the computer or pen a letter. Have a list of questions you want to ask, and keep it handy. If the conversation turns to an exciting hunt or goes down a side track, the prospective hunter may hang up having enjoyed his conversation but failed to get the pertinent information he needs to make an informed decision.

Don't be afraid to ask questions. It's your money, and you want to spend it wisely. Ask exactly and specifically what the hunt costs and includes. Ground transportation, license fees, and meat handling are just some of the expenses that could be included in a package or could be optional.

What kind of questions should you ask? Your initial questions should be brief and to the point: What services does he provide? When is the best time to hunt in his area? How many hunters take how many bears annually? Stick to the basics, and once you have narrowed your selection to several possible guides, ask for more specific information.

Here are some questions a radical bear hunter should ask a prospective guide before deciding to book a hunt. I have compiled these questions over the years, and they are the questions I ask before I choose a guide. Many of the questions will lead to additional questions in an attempt to seek enough information to decide which operation will suit your needs best.

Bait hunts—If you plan on going on a bait hunt, ask how many active baits the guide maintains each season and what the bait-to-hunter ratio is. The guide should have at least three baits for each hunter in camp annually. For example, if the guide has a total of twenty-five hunters annually, he should have seventy-five active baits. This gives the hunter options if

When baits are set up improperly, bears will knock over the barrel, remove the bait, and run into the cover to eat it. This drastically reduces shot opportunities.

something goes bad at one of the baits. Also ask when he starts baiting. Many guides start baiting only about a week or so before the first group of hunters arrive in camp. Such baits are not really active until the third or fourth group arrives, so if you are in the first group you could be disappointed. The baits should be started well before the bears come out of the den, should be checked daily until hit, and then should be replenished daily. Find out if baits are rehunted by other hunters. I will not hunt a bait behind another hunter because I have no idea what kind of hunter he was or what he did while on the stand.

Also check on how often baits are reloaded and what bait is used. The baits should be checked and refilled around the same time each day. The bears become programmed, and after awhile filling the bait will be like the dinner bell going off. Find out what is used for bait, and make sure it is something the bears like and that will have them coming back daily to check for goodies. Also ask about the average number of bears seen on a daily basis. The average should be one a day, because some days hunters see two bears and other days they see none.

You should know how far apart the baits are. The home range of a mature bear is large, and if the baits are only a few miles apart the same bears could be hitting multiple baits. Furthermore if the baits are relatively close to one another, most likely the guide has been hunting the area for several years, and chances are he has taken most of the mature animals out of the population. Lastly, ask how the baits are accessed. From my experience, the best ones are accessed by water because they usually are more remote.

Hunting with hounds—Before choosing this exciting type of hunt, ask the guide whether hunting with dogs is legal where you plan to go. Then ask about the hounds. Experienced and well-trained dogs are critical to a successful hunt behind bear hounds. Find out if any of the dogs are new to the pack or if any were lost recently or last season. A new dog thrown into the pack, especially a young one, could make a big difference on a mean old bear that continually bays up on the ground. Also if one or more of the best hounds has been removed from the pack for one reason or the other, it can dramatically affect how the chase goes. Dogs that are not fully trained or experienced can result in a disappointing experience.

When an area is overhunted, smaller animals are harvested.

Find out more about the area where the hunt takes place. If the area does not have a good road system, you may have to spend a lot of time on foot once the chase has started to get to the treed bear. Many times these hunts can be extremely demanding physically, especially if you end up chasing a big old boar that continually bays up on the ground. Make sure you are physically up to the task.

Spot and stalk hunt—For this type of hunt, ask how many bears are typically seen on a daily basis. How the hunting areas will be accessed is also important. Many operations are boat- or vehicle-based and once you spot an animal, you'll attempt the stalk. Some of these hunts may be physically demanding, and the hunter must be in good physical shape to climb steep mountains and plow through thick underbrush for long distances. Be prepared for disappointments because missed attempts on a stalk are common, especially for a bowhunter.

Hunt specifics—Whatever method the hunter chooses for his hunt, he should find out how large the area is that he will be hunting. This is very important. Many guides only have a relatively small hunting area, and if they have hunted it hard for several years the hunters will be taking mostly immature three- and four-year-old bears on their hunts. It takes over seven years for a boar to mature fully even in excellent habitat, so only if a guide has vast areas at his disposal can a hunter be ensured opportunities to harvest a mature animal. The good guides that I know who have vast hunting areas will rotate the areas hunted every couple years so their clients have access to mature bears. This is much the same as a farmer rotating his crops in fields to ensure better growth.

How many hunters does the guide take each season? How many on a weekly basis? I prefer small operations that take no more than four hunters per week and can cater to my needs on the hunt rather than a big operation that is only concerned with taking in numbers of hunters. Dollar for dollar, the small operations usually will give the hunter a much better quality hunt. Also find out how many total hunters visit the area per year, especially in areas with two-bear limits. Most of the bigger operations take more bears per year, but the quality of the animals taken is not as good.

What is considered a trophy bear in the hunting area? Many areas produce bigger and better bears than other areas. Don't be too concerned with the bear's weight since it can vary depending on the time of year. Instead, ask about the average hide length, nose to tail, of the bears taken. A 6-foot bear, nose to tail, is a trophy anywhere. What is the skull size of the average animal taken? A boar with an 18-inch skull is a mature animal that any hunter would be proud of taking. If you are interested in a color-phase bear, ask what colors are available and what percentage of hunters have an opportunity at these bears.

What is the guide's annual success rate per hunter or—better yet—the hunter's rate or percentage of opportunity? A hunter should never expect anything more than an opportunity at a quality animal on any type of hunt. If the guide provides that opportunity, he has done his job and should not be held accountable for any hunter who literally blows his chance at a good bear. Every year, we hear stories about the missed shots. I have missed myself, and if I told you differently I would be lying. Keep in mind that sometimes guides will try to push a client into taking a smaller animal just to inflate their overall success rate.

Also check on the lodging side of the operation. Tents, cabins, lodges, a camp cook, and hot showers may sound incidental, but after a long sit in foul weather a hot shower and a well-cooked meal will do much to revive a flagging hunter.

Trophy care—Find out about trophy care of the animal. Does the guide skin the bear for the hunter? Skinning a bear correctly can be difficult for the hunter who has never done it before, and this inexperience could run the risk of ruining the bear hide. Will the hide be salted or frozen? Either way is fine, but I prefer freezing because if the hide is not salted properly the hair will start to pull and the hide could be ruined. Also ask what paperwork is required to take the animal home. Many places require paperwork to transport your hide and meat across state lines or over the border from Canada. Some guides will offer the services of a taxidermist and deliver the hide to him; they also may ship the finished product right to your door. How does the guide handle the meat? Do they simply quarter it for the hunter or can it be butchered? The meat from a bear can be delicious and should not be wasted, even if the hunter has to donate the meat.

Before you go—Find out what distances you should be practicing on the target range with your weapon of choice. Depending on the method of hunting used, the hunter could be required to make a shot as far away as three hundred yards or as close as ten yards, on the ground or from an elevated position. You want to be ready when the moment of truth arises. Also find out if Sunday hunting is allowed, and if not, if fishing is available. You'll know whether to pack a rod to fill that empty day and to make arrangements for a fishing license, if you need one.

If you feel insecure about arranging a hunt yourself, consider using a booking agent to arrange a hunt through a reputable guiding service. It's simple and relatively painless: Tell the booking agent what type of hunt you want, and he will make all the arrangements. Just like a travel agent, most agents receive a commission from the guide, so there usually is no extra cost incurred by the hunter, but check just to be sure.

Reference—Don't hesitate to ask for several references. Then once you've obtained a list of names of previous clients, follow up and contact them. Word of mouth is important in the guiding business, and recommendations from friends or other hunters who have been to a certain camp can give you invaluable firsthand information about what to expect, how the camp is operated, and how they'd rate the proficiency of the guides. A good reference from a satisfied but unsuccessful hunter says much more about a guide than one from someone who managed to take an animal but may not have received the professional services they paid for. Any professional should be happy to provide this information. Guides expect a hunter to ask for references, and they hope that they may use your name in the future if you book a successful hunt with them. Don't assume that just because a guide has given you a name, it must be a good camp or a well-run operation. Follow up with the references; they are an all-important source of information.

TRUSTING YOUR GUIDE

Once you arrive in camp and your eagerly awaited hunt is about to begin, trust your guide. Have faith in his ability and follow his advice. Let him lead the hunt; after all, he is the one in the woods with the bear population day after day. You have paid for his experience and expertise, and it is foolish not to follow his instructions and judgment. Many times hunters don't give enough credit to a guide and will want to run the show themselves.

Although guides do their best to get every hunter a shot at a good bear, in all fairness it does not occur all the time. Circumstances such as weather, hunting pressure, and the nature of the bears are things he cannot control. Guides are human too, and they can make mistakes. If that happens, it's unfortunate, but a hunter should not expect superhuman results from a guide. To avoid this disappointment, consider booking a longer hunt of seven to nine days to allow more flexibility. Hunters who book short trips limit their chances of success—a five-day hunt may have rain the entire period, for example—although often this will be enough time to harvest a trophy bear in a good camp with an experienced guide.

If you don't see much action on the first couple of days of hunting, don't become discouraged. Positive attitude and attention to every detail of good hunting techniques are important for any hunt to succeed. A hunter must be persistent and confident in the guide and himself and let the bears do the rest.

Planning a bear hunt can be as easy as picking up the phone to call a booking agent or as involved as planning the hunt yourself. In either case, the radical bear hunter must do his homework and check those references. The process can be time-consuming, but it can reap huge benefits in terms of knowledge and satisfaction, especially for the hunter who capitalizes on the skills of a professional guide to help put him in the best possible position for bringing down a trophy bear. If you put in a little effort up front, you'll lessen the chances of your dream hunt turning into a nightmare.

CHAPTER 14

Do-it-Yourself Trophy Bear Hunting

Planning a black bear hunt on a limited budget can be a frustrating experience. The typical hunter will collect a few magazine ads and brochures from sport shows and then contact the outfitters that sound good to him. When they do, they realize there is nothing inexpensive about a guided bear hunt; prices range from $2,000 to more than $4,000 per hunter, and that doesn't include tags and transportation to the location. And the times are changing. It is becoming increasingly more expensive each year to hunt black bear. But black bear hunts can be had for those individuals who search out hidden deals.

In many places in black bear country, you don't need to go through an outfitter to bag your bear. The radical bear hunter will give you a lifetime of tips, including how to pick the best time and place to hunt, to assure you of a successful bear hunt.

The black bear hunter today faces numerous challenges when planning a hunt, whether it's close to home or in a distant place. Concerns include limited access to private lands, the inflated price of trespass fees, and reduced opportunities to hunt on public land because of quotas on the harvest and limited license drawings. Although a fully guided hunt can tackle most of these issues, the overall cost of the hunt can be prohibitive to many individuals. There are other, less talked about alternatives for the bear hunter. The "do-it-yourself hunt" where the hunter is not guided or is brought to a drop camp could be the right choice for many hunters.

If you have always dreamed of going on a black bear hunt but never really pursued it because of the cost or the amount of work involved, this type of hunt may be right for you. Any individual can plan and take the black bear hunt of a lifetime without breaking the bank to hire a quality guide service. It will only take a small amount of your savings and lots of research and fortitude to make that dream black bear hunt a reality.

Some unguided bear hunters will always do better than others. Sometimes, it's luck. Other times, it's a matter of having a positive attitude and a willingness to hunt up to the last minute of the last day no matter how tough the hunting has been. A do-it-yourself hunt is not everyone's cup of tea, and only hunters with extensive hunting experience should consider going on an unguided hunting trip. But a hunter with a lot of experience typically will do well on an unguided black bear hunt and generally will be quite successful.

PLANNING A "DO-IT-YOURSELF" HUNT

After having hunted the black bear for more than thirty-five years, I've developed a certain amount of confidence and independence in my ability to hunt these big furry critters anywhere across their North American range. For that reason, I believe that if a radical bear hunter pursues my easy-to-follow instructional tips, he can set up a quality black bear hunt on his own that will be a rewarding experience.

Start early with your planning. I can't emphasize that enough to any hunter who wants to go on a do-it-yourself bear hunt. I recommend starting to plan the adventure at least one year in advance.

Choosing the Destination

The first decision the hunter has to make is where to hunt. In choosing a destination, consider license costs, bear density, the potential for a trophy bear, the hunter success rate, the type of terrain, distance of travel, and total costs.

The best place to start looking for locations for the hunt are wildlife agencies' Web sites. Many of these Web sites include priceless information, such as harvest statistics and percentage of hunter success by region or management area, bear densities, and the amount of average hunting days to harvest a bear. The hunter should take all of this collected data and study it carefully, weighing what each of the locations has to offer and how they will fit with the hunter's objective. These same Web sites will include other basic information such as license fees, information about quota systems or draws, and season dates. Armed with this information, the hunter should be able to make an extremely educated choice on what location will meet his overall objective for the type of hunt he desires.

Let Your Fingers Do the Walking

Now that the hunter has chosen the location for his hunt, it is time to let his fingers do the walking by picking up the telephone and making a few calls. A good place to start is to speak to the bear biologist who oversees the location of the planned hunting area. Try calling the main information telephone number of the wildlife agency and ask for the name and extension number of the bear biologist. The hunter should have prepared specific questions to ask the biologist before calling. Ask about estimates of the bear population by management area, food preferences during the time of the planned hunt, which areas have the less hunting pressure, which areas seem to produce the largest animals each season, and the bears' sex ratio estimates. Wildlife biologists are bombarded with calls regularly from individuals looking for the best places to hunt. From my experience of working with these professionals over the years, if the hunter is courteous and asks intelligent questions that show he has carefully done his homework, most biologists will be willing to give detailed information about the bears.

Another good source is the local conservation officer; this person will know as much about the area as anyone and should be able to fill in a few holes. I also like to contact the local taxidermist in the area. Many times this person can be a wealth of information on where the biggest bears are taken annually. Lastly, it is a good idea to speak with foresters who spend lots of time in the area. They will know of locations where trees have been cut recently that will provide a food magnet for bears.

Search Out Other Hunters

A hunter who has firsthand experience hunting an area can be a valuable resource of information. Start by asking the owners of local sporting goods stores, the local taxidermist, motel owners, and local gas station employees. Also check within your circle of friends to see if one may know of a person that has hunted a certain location. Another great source of information is the forums on the many hunting-related Web sites available today. If the hunter works hard at it, in most cases he should be able to find someone who will be able to provide a few tips about an area.

Set a Realistic Budget

Very few hunters have unlimited funds to spend on a trip. For most of us, every nickel counts, so a hunter should work out a sensible budget that will fit his needs. No one wants to realize at the last minute that he won't have enough money to cover the trip. Start by writing down all the basic expenditures of the hunting trip, always figuring on the high side to provide a cushion. Include expenses such as airfare or fuel costs if driving, accommodations, food, license fees, and a sundry that could cover anything unforeseen that may occur, such as vehicle breakdowns or repairs, a

Decide for yourself if you want to rough it in a tent camp.

forgotten item that needs to be purchased, and the processing of meat, if you are successful at harvesting a bear. Planning for every expense that could pop up on a trip is impossible, but the point is to give enough of a buffer for any reasonable expense that may occur. If something out of the ordinary happens and you are short of cash, use that Visa card as a backup.

Be in Good Shape for the Hunt

If you want to tip the odds in your favor, make sure you are physically up to the sometimes rigorous demands of a hunt. Many bear hunts can be physically demanding, and if the hunter is out of shape for the hunt, he will have a miserable time. Every hunter should prepare for the expected conditions he'll encounter on a hunt by starting an extensive exercise program well in advance of the trip. Before beginning an exercise program, a physical examination by a doctor is highly recommended.

Actual Hunting Time

Most hunters simply don't allow themselves enough time of actual hunting days on their trip to be successful. They take a week off work, but by the time they either drive or fly back and forth to the location they end up with only four or five days of actual hunting time. I realize that most people only have so much vacation time they can take away from their job

Some places will let you stay at their lodge and hunt DIY (do-it-yourself).

Many outfitters offer DIY hunts that include lodging and meals.

and family, but if the hunter can be a little flexible with his time, he would increase his odds for success. On a fully guided hunt, four or five days may be enough time, but for the do-it-yourself hunt, you will need more time in most situations. I like to have a minimum of seven hunting days, and with the proper planning most individuals can arrange for that, too. If the hunter takes a week off from work, he will have a total of nine days, counting the weekends at the beginning and end of the week. If he can add just one more day to his trip, he would have a total of ten days, giving him three days for travel and setting up and breaking down camp. And if he is lucky enough to fill his tag early, he can head home ahead of schedule.

Proper Attitude
All hunters should go into their hunt with the proper attitude and remember to have fun. Isn't the pleasure we get out of a hunt the real reason every one of us hunts? Take the time to relax and create some lasting memories of the experience. I know everyone wants to kill a monster bear and if we said we didn't we would not be honest with ourselves, but we need to keep our expectations within reason. Many years ago, Glen St.

Charles, the founder of the Pope and Young Club, told me something that I never will forget. He said that all hunts should be measured by the effort one puts into it, rather than what one gets out of it.

I vividly remember many years ago trekking to northern Ontario, Canada, with a group for a spring bear hunt and to train young hounds. At the time, there was no limit on the number of bears one could harvest. The hunter just had to purchase another tag for a few dollars from the Ministry of Natural Resources. We had a ball camping, fishing, and hunting bears in that vast country, and some of my greatest memories sharing good times with friends occurred in that northern wilderness. We had lots of fun together shooting a few really nice bears and letting many more go. We enjoyed the experience together and never set unreasonable expectations that would put pressure on us. If you make having a safe and memorable experience on your bear hunting trip a priority, you will never be disappointed, and a big bear will merely be the frosting on the cake.

MY PICKS FOR THE BEST DO-IT-YOURSELF HUNTS

The hunter can venture to a great many places for an unguided do-it-yourself bear hunt, but I recommend the following locations for their reasonable costs and high success rates. Some tags are available over the counter in certain states or Canadian provinces. Other states and provinces only issue the tags through a limited entry draw or lottery process, so it is best to check before finalizing trip plans. It is also a good idea to check on season dates since many places only have a fall bear hunting season.

Prince of Wales Island, Alaska—Here, on the third largest island in the United States, almost the entire isle is open to the public for hunting. Over the last few decades, the U.S. Forest Service has done many logging operations, which have opened up areas that were virtually impenetrable. This logging also created almost two thousand miles of logging roads that are open for use to the public.

Black bears wander everywhere on the island which is part of the Tongass National Forest. It's a spot and stalk hunter's paradise, and the success rates are exceptionally high. Another plus is the two-bag limit. Although the hunter has a choice to hunt either spring or fall seasons, all the bears are black in color.

Ferries run several times daily to the island, and the hunter can either rent a vehicle on the mainland to take over on the ferry or rent one on the island, which in most cases is more economical. Remote cabins scattered across the island rent for as little as $25 per day, and a few motels and bed and breakfasts offer additional accommodations.

Float planes can be chartered to get to remote locations.

Not only is Prince of Wales Island the bargain basement of quality do-it-yourself black bear hunts, but it provides a great opportunity to take a trophy bear in one of the last true frontiers remaining in North America today.

Alaska Department of Fish and Game

907-465-4190

www.adfg.state.ak.us

Arizona—Arizona has big bears in nice color phases. The state offers the self-guided hunter an excellent opportunity for success. For the hunter who wants to increase his chances, a few operations within the state offer prehunt scouting packages and maps. The packages are geared to the hunter's individual needs and wants and compared to a fully guided hunt in the state for black bear, which can cost upwards of $5,000 per person, are a real bargain. The package costs approximately $500, which if divided among four hunters would be a bargain at $125 each.

Beware of operations that offer scouting packages as a sideline to fully guided hunts. Who do you think will get the prime areas to hunt—

their high-priced guided hunters or the guy who paid the small scouting fee? But finding the right scouting package can be money well spent. The state doesn't have a huge population of bears roaming, but wildlife officials have done a good job managing the animals. In the areas around Flagstaff, which have good bear densities, the success rates are higher for the do-it-yourself hunter.

Arizona Game and Fish
602-942-3000
www.gf.state.az.us

Maine—This eastern state, which has a good black bear population, has only a relatively long fall season to hunt bears. All of the hunting methods are legal, but bait is the most productive for the self-guided hunter unless he has a pack of hounds to chase a bear. Many operations offer reasonable packages for the do-it-yourself adventure hunter in the north woods. For under $600 per hunter, you can get set up in a campsite (you will have to bring your own tent, trailer or RV) with prebaited areas and a guide to show you the locations of the stands when you arrive. You will be given enough bait for the week, plus instructions on what and what not to do, and then the rest is up to you. Most operators will not charge a fee for additional nonhunting family members.

The success rates for the do-it-yourself hunt in Maine are not exceptional for really good bears; the average bear is somewhere around 125 and 150 pounds. But for the hunter who lives in the East, can drive there in a day, and just wants an opportunity at a black bear, Maine can be a real bargain. Many hunters will combine a deer and bear hunting trip to the north woods of Maine in hopes of getting a crack at both animals.

Maine Department of Inland Fisheries and Wildlife
207-287-8000
www.maine.gov/ifw

Montana—The Big Sky country has lots of black bears, especially in the areas north and west of Missoula. Only spot and stalk hunting is legal in the state, but the terrain is very conducive to this method. The hunter can spot bears from his vehicle and plan a stalk; the state has virtually hundreds of miles of logging roads, of which many are gated and closed to traffic, where the hunter can walk the roads looking for an animal. Look for areas that have been logged recently that make feeding bears easier to see. The state does not have a reputation for monster bears, but it has a good percentage of color-phase animals. The many national forests and public campgrounds can provide an affordable base camp for the

Maine bear harvested while on a do-it-yourself hunt.

hunter. The do-it-yourself bear hunter can have reasonably good success harvesting a bear in this state at an affordable price with breathtaking views.

Montana Fish Wildlife and Parks
406-444-2612
www.fwp.mt.gov/

New Hampshire—The Granite State may be the most overlooked bear hunting place in the Northeast for the do-it-yourself bear hunter. Not only does New Hampshire have affordable prices, but the state has quality animals, a long fall season, and great bear habitat. All three popular methods of pursuing bears are legal, and the state experiences almost no bear hunting pressure. From my experience, the average size of New Hampshire bears is much larger than bears in the other states in the region. In the White Mountain region, the bear per square mile ratio is almost one. This vast area has a great road system for gaining access to the back country and contains many campgrounds for the hunter to pop up his tent or

Two happy hunters with a New Hampshire bear they harvested while hunting out of a tent campground.

trailer. The most productive methods are baiting and hounds, if you have them. Most hunters use the baiting method, but they will need time to get the baits established in a prime area if they want to achieve success on their hunt.

Plan on a two-week hunt in this area, and go later in the season so that the baits will not be competing with natural feeds, such as berries, and agricultural crops, such as corn and apples.

If the hunter wants to hunt from a stand, early season is best. Look for standing corn or apple orchards, and ask the farmers if they have seen bear damage to their crops. Then ask if you can hunt on their land. Most farmers will allow access because they despise the extensive damage bears create each season. This can be a productive method of hunting bears in this country. Since the crops are just like bait without the work, it will require much less time than baiting on your own.

New Hampshire Fish and Game Department
603-271-2461
www.wildlife.state.nh.us

Ontario—This centrally located Canadian province is large and boasts high black bear densities in several areas. It is one of two Canadian provinces that do not have a spring bear season. The spring season was

Dick harvested this blackie on an Ontario do-it-yourself hunt in the late 1980s.

eliminated several years ago after several antihunting groups applied pressure. Since then, the territory has experienced an upsurge in the bear density in many areas. The increase in bear population has created problems with predation on other wildlife species, such as moose during spring calving, and caused other bear nuisance incidents.

The fall season usually runs about ten weeks starting in mid-August. The province allows all three popular methods of hunting bears and is one of the few places where a crossbow is a legal weapon.

Baiting is the most popular and productive method of bear hunting for the do-it-yourself hunter, and the success rates can run as high as seventy percent in good areas. Several operations cater to the self-guided hunter with prebaited sites. This arrangement can be a great option for the hunter who does not have a few weeks to get bears coming to his own baits. Many operations will even allow the hunter to stay at their lodge or rent a cabin with or without meals for a nominal fee. Unless the hunter has the time to spend getting the actual bait together and establishing the site, he should consider the prebaited option.

The area around Lake Nipigon, especially on the north side of the lake, habitually produces a few good animals every year. Also don't overlook the vast wilderness around Sioux Lookout, which has exceptional bear habitat and a high bear density.

Ontario Ministry of Natural Resources
800-667-1940
www.mnr.gov.on.ca.MNR

Quebec—This eastern Canadian province has a healthy black bear population distributed across the entire land mass. The hunter does not have to go to the far north to find a bear. As a matter of fact, most of the better bear densities are in the central and southern regions of the province. The areas around Algonquin Provincial Park in the south have habitually produced several nice bears each year. I also like the area around Chiboqamau, especially to the north and east of Mistassini Provincial Reserve. For the hunter who likes to wet a line, fishing can be a real bonus in this area.

The province offers both spring and fall seasons to hunt black bear, and the seasons are quite long. Baiting is the most productive method for the do-it-yourself hunter, and the success rates run about seventy percent in the spring and drop to about fifty to sixty percent in the fall because of competing natural feed availability. During the spring season, however, the hunter can really get hammered with insects. The bears on average are smaller than expected, with weights running between 100 and 150 pounds. Larger bears have been taken, but they are the exception rather than the rule.

Many outfitters in the state offer prebaited, self-guided packages that include cabins on lakes with fishing and boat rentals available. The costs are reasonable, and such a trip could be turned into a family vacation. Don't expect to see many monster bears here, because they are few and far between. The province also doesn't have any color phases available. The bears are as black as coal.

Quebec Ministry of Natural Resources
418-627-8600
www.mnr.gouv.qc.ca/english/home.jsp

CHAPTER 15

Live Smart in Black Bear Country

Nothing compares to the feeling a bear hunter gets when he stumbles upon deep massive pad and claw bear tracks pressed into the earth. They are a symbol of the wilderness in North America. To me, the black bear is dignity and supremacy matched by no other animal except a grizzly bear. The dense fur of its thick black robe rippling over powerful muscles as the bear slowly meanders through the wilderness is a sight to behold.

But as more of us build homes and cabins and recreate in bear country, conflicts between humans and bears are increasing. Also with increasing bear populations, the bears' home range has expanded into places where we haven't seen bears for years.

Seeing a wild bear is an exciting and memorable experience. When visiting, recreating, or living in or near black bear country, be aware that you may encounter a bear at any time. Most black bears are wary of humans and will usually leave when encountered. Although seeing a bear can be a memorable experience, many people are terrified when they encounter a bear. Black bears after all are capable of aggressive behavior. The black bear also is much more curious and adaptable than any other type of bear. It can quickly become accustomed to human activity and as it develops aggressive food-seeking habits, it can be dangerous. Black bears have been known to stalk and actually kill humans.

When in the woods, we are responsible for our own safety and the safety of the bears. We must keep black bears wild by not approaching or feeding them. We also must try to reduce conflicts between bears and humans if we want to avoid the unnecessary loss of bears and maintain support from the nonhunting public for sound bear management. We all must "be bear aware" by learning effective measures to prevent bear problems. Awareness and prevention strategies will help both bears and humans.

The best way to avoid bear problems is not to attract the animals in the first place. Although a bear can become accustomed to humans, it is still a wild animal, no matter how domesticated it appears. Bears are not a family pet or a teddy bear that you can hug and cuddle. You must always be cautious around black bears because they can react very unpredictably.

The reminder of this chapter gives you tips for living in black bear country. If you follow these simple guidelines, you will save yourself many problems and reduce the incidents that would cause a bear to become a nuisance and have to be destroyed.

UNDERSTANDING BEAR BEHAVIOR

- Startled bears often will confront intruders by turning sideways to appear larger, making woofing and teeth clacking sounds, salivating, laying their ears back, and slapping the ground with their paws.
- Mother bears are very protective of their cubs. A startled sow will often send her cubs up a tree while she stands guard at the bottom. This gives the person an opportunity to leave without a confrontation. Mother bears try to avoid people, but if surprised they might bluff charge to remove the threat.
- If a bear stands on its hind feet, it is not being aggressive. It is trying to see, hear, and smell the intruder so it can identify what it is in front of it.
- During extreme conditions such as droughts, thunderstorms, and forest fires, all wildlife, especially bears, may become more visible, aggressive, or confrontational.
- If you come across a bear, detour as far away as possible while monitoring the bear's behavior. If the bear is close to the trail and you are unable to bypass it or return the way you came, wait for the bear to leave the trail area. If the bear is approaching, it is best to identify yourself as a human by allowing the bear to see and hear what you are. The bear then should divert its direction to avoid the human.

SURVIVING A CLOSE ENCOUNTER WITH A BEAR

- If you encounter a bear, do not panic. Group together, pick up any small children, and assess the situation. Prepare to use bear spray.
- Do not run or make sudden movements as it may instinctively cause the bear to charge.
- Give bears a chance to identify you as a human and not a threat. If the bear stands up, it is trying to see, hear, and smell you better. Talk firmly in a low-pitched voice while backing away. Avoid direct eye contact as bears may perceive this as a challenge or threat.

Nobody wants to be eye-to-eye with a bear like this! CUDDEBACK DIGITAL

- Continue to back away slowly and cautiously, retreating to a place of safety. Monitor the bear's response, and adjust actions accordingly.
- Recognize that any bear that continues to approach, follow, disappear and reappear, or display other stalking behaviors is acting in a predatory manner. Bears that attack people in a tent or confront them aggressively in their campsite or cooking area should also be considered a predatory threat.
- If the bear does not respond to aggressive actions, such as yelling or throwing rocks and sticks, and it attempts to make contact, be prepared to fight back. If you have bear spray, emit a deterring blast, preferably when the bear is about twenty-five feet away. This gives the animal time to divert its advance. Save enough spray for a full blast in the face when he is closer.

TRAVELING IN BEAR COUNTRY

Whether you hike, mountain bike, float rivers, or ride horses, you should take several precautions whenever you are in a bear habitat environment. Following the suggestions below will help make the journey safer for you, your companions, and the bears. Remember all bears can be dangerous. Do not for any reason approach or feed wild bears.

Common Causes of Bear Attacks While Hiking
- Not making sufficient noise.
- Approaching or surprising a bear at close range.
- Getting close to a carcass or other food source.
- Startling a female bear with cubs.
- Hiking off trail or at night.

Reduce the Risk of Close Encounters
- Let someone know where you are going and when you will return.
- Keep children close to you and within your immediate sight at all times.
- Make noise by talking, singing, or clapping your hands to let the bear know of your presence. Don't rely on bells; usually they are too quiet. Shout often, especially when traveling upwind near streams and waterfalls or when you cannot see the path ahead because of thick brush.
- Be alert and always watch for bear sign, such as tracks, droppings, rocks rolled over, scratch marks on trees, and logs torn apart. Carry binoculars and scan ahead periodically. Keep bear spray readily available.
- Don't hike alone or at night. Bears are most active at dawn, dusk, and night, but they can be encountered at any time. Groups make noise and appear more formidable than a solo hiker.
- Stay on trails both for your safety and to protect the habitat.
- Avoid carcasses you encounter and report any dead animals to the nearest ranger station or game warden. It is risky to approach a carcass because a bear may be just out of sight, guarding its food.
- Avoid odorous items, such as food and beverages with strong odors, scented deodorants and lotions, and any other odorous items from home. A bear's acute sense of smell can detect smells from great distances. Dry foods are both less odorous and lighter to carry.
- Stay with your gear. Don't leave your packs, food, or beverages unattended; even food or beverages stored under water may attract a bear.
- Avoid taking pets on hiking trails. Pets may attract bears, and they are not allowed on trails in our national parks and refuges. If dogs are permitted in an area, keep them on a short leash to avoid conflicts with bears.
- View and photograph bears from established observation areas or the trail. If a bear approaches, back away to maintain a safe distance.

If you come face-to-face with a bear in bear country, be sure to follow Be Bear Aware guidelines. CUDDEBACK DIGITAL

- Use binoculars, spotting scopes, or a telephoto lens to view and photograph a bear. Keeping your distance will avoid stressing the animal.
- When biking and running, carefully select the areas you will be recreating in and be extra alert in bear country. Speed and quick movements increase the risk of a sudden encounter.
- Hike at a pace everyone can maintain and stay together. Some bears behave in a predatory manner and will seek out the easiest target. Don't hike ahead or allow someone to fall behind, especially children and pets.
- Climb a tree only if it is near and the bear is far away. Running to a tree may provoke a bear to chase you, and you cannot outrun a bear. Bears can run up to thirty miles per hour, up and downhill. Keep in mind that all black bears climb trees.
- Always follow local regulations and review trailhead signs before entering an area.

BACKCOUNTRY CAMPING
- Set up cooking, eating, and supply areas at least a hundred yards from your sleeping area. Hang food and odorous items at least ten

to fifteen feet above ground and four feet from top and side supports, or store it in an approved, bear-resistant container.

- Select food sold in individually sealed packages. Plan meals carefully to prevent leftovers.
- Store pet food, livestock feed, and garbage the same as food. Never bury it; always pack it out.
- Strain food particles from dishwater by using a fine-mesh screen and store the particles with garbage. Dump dishwater at least a hundred yards from your sleeping area. Food odors may attract bears.
- Keep sleeping bags and tents completely free of food, food odors, and beverages.
- Store personal items such as deodorants, toothpaste, soap, and lotions with food and garbage when not in use. Any odorous product may attract bears.
- Camp in open areas away from trails, thick brush, berry patches, spawning streams, or animal carcasses. Sleep in a tent for increased safety.
- Keep a flashlight and bear spray readily available.
- Wash your hands after cooking, eating, or handling fish or game to minimize odors.
- Do not sleep in the clothes you cook or handle game or fish in.
- Rehearse what you and others in your group will do, day or night, if a bear appears in your camp or while you're hiking. Always review the local regulations.

If a bear enters your campsite or your sleeping and cooking areas seeking food, it is acting in a predatory manner. Group together and retreat to a place of safety. If yelling and throwing things from a distance does not cause the bear to retreat, leave the area immediately. Report the incident to the local wildlife management agency, and retrieve your personal belongings with its assistance. If a bear attacks you or a companion in your campsite or eating area, consider it a predatory confrontation and aggressively fight back with everything possible.

STAYING IN MANAGED CAMPGROUNDS

- Don't be careless with food or garbage when camping; bears may wander through a campsite at any time of day or night. Wild bears near a campground are more likely to be habituated or food-conditioned and—having lost their fear of humans—are often increasingly aggressive in their attempts to obtain human, pet, and livestock food.

- Keep a clean camp to protect yourself and others and to prevent wild bears from obtaining human food and garbage. Deposit all garbage in wildlife-resistant trash containers.
- Store all food and food-related items inside a closed, hard-sided vehicle or special bear-resistant container except when preparing or eating food. Ice chests, coolers, boxes, cans, tents, and soft-sided campers are not bear resistant!
- Store pet food and livestock feed in the same manner as human food, out of reach from bears.
- Keep pets on a leash or inside a cool, well-ventilated vehicle. Pets may threaten and harass bears and can entice predators to your camp. Pets are not allowed on hiking trails in most parks and refuges. Do not leave pets unattended in bear country.
- When walking in a campground at night, always carry bear spray, use a flashlight, and stay alert.
- Ask campers who are not observing precautions to clean up their camp for the safety of others, both visitors and bears.
- Remove all food and garbage from campground storage boxes before you leave.
- Use a designated camping area and set up tents with space between them.
- Keep a flashlight and bear spray readily available.
- Never assume bears traveling through campgrounds are tame, and never approach or feed one.
- Immediately notify the campground host if you encounter a bear near your campground area.

BEING BEAR AWARE IN RESIDENTIAL AREAS

- Minimize odors and the availability of food rewards throughout your yard and neighborhood. Report all residential bear encounters to your local wildlife management agency and police department, and notify your neighbors of the situation.
- Remove any dense brush that could provide cover for a bear and make a surprise encounter likely.
- If a bear repeatedly enters your yard, determine what attractants are drawing it there and remove them immediately.
- Put out garbage on the day of pickup, not the night before. Store in a sturdy building or place in an approved bear-resistant trash receptacle.
- Do not leave pet food out. Hang bird feeders out of a bear's reach, and take them down during periods of high bear activity.

When encountering a bear in close proximity, follow the Be Bear Aware guidelines. CUDDEBACK DIGITAL

- Keep barbeques clean and grease free. Store livestock/pet feed and other attractants inside a sturdy building.
- Pick all ripe fruit from fruit trees and off the surrounding ground.
- Do not put meat, fish, and other pungent scraps in compost piles. Add lime to compost piles to reduce odor and accelerate decomposition.
- Consider installing an electric fence to keep bears out of orchards, gardens, compost piles, and beehives. Always follow appropriate safety precautions.
- Do not attempt to chase or harass a bear out of your yard. All bears can be dangerous. Contact the appropriate authority for assistance.
- Consider the time of year. Bear activity may intensify in spring when bears are hungry and emerging from their dens, in the fall when bears are bulking up for hibernation, and during drought periods when natural foods are often scare.

BEAR-SMART COMMUNITIES

Throughout North America, wildlife management specialists and conservation and police officers respond to thousands of calls and complaints about bears. Most of these problems are a direct result of bears obtaining food rewards throughout a community. Unfortunately, these bears are often destroyed in an effort to protect people and property.

A friend had to remove this deer feeder from his backyard because of bear problems. CUDDEBACK DIGITAL

By establishing a wildlife stewardship campaign, an entire community can cooperatively help reduce human/wildlife conflicts. To spread the word, student youth groups, city and county agencies, and neighborhood groups can work together to distribute educational and public awareness materials to visitors and new residents.

Tips for a Wildlife-Smart Community

- Assemble a group of volunteers and prepare an assessment of the wildlife hazards in your community and surrounding area. Work closely with your local wildlife management agency.
- Prepare a wildlife/human conflict management plan that addresses the wildlife hazards and land use conflicts identified in the previous step.
- Establish local bylaws that prohibit the provision of food to wildlife, whether as a result of intent, neglect, or irresponsible management of attractants. Assist in planning new housing developments so that greenbelts don't channel wildlife through populated areas.
- Conduct a continuing wildlife education program directed at all sectors of the community. Involve youth groups and students who can help conduct workshops and training programs among their peers.

Cubs playing in a neighbor's backyard. CUDDEBACK DIGITAL

- Clean brush away from playgrounds, schools, and other areas where children actively play.
- Establish a community response system for notifying neighbors and authorities of wildlife that may be dangerous in the community.
- Develop and maintain a bear-proof municipal solid waste management system. Design trash-transfer centers that are out in the open and visible by passing traffic. Remove all grass or brush from the area. Provide strong fencing that extends below the ground surface. Keep the area free of trash. Restaurants, packinghouses, and other sources of highly attractive garbage should also use bear-resistant dumpsters.

HUNTING IN BEAR COUNTRY
Hunting in bear country requires special equipment, skills, and precautions. Properly prepare for your hunt by using these checklists.

Special Equipment Checklist:
- EPA-registered bear spray. Every hunter in the group should have at least one canister.
- Pulley systems and ropes for food storage and hanging game meat.
- Drop cloth for relocating game.
- Gloves and apron for handling game.

- Cell phone or handheld two-way radio.
- First aid kit.
- Most recent food storage and game handling regulations.

On the Hunt

- Always be aware of your surroundings. Scan ahead, beside you, and behind you. Bears can be hard to see. Also remember you may not be the only hunter out there.
- Let someone know where you are hunting and when you will return.
- Avoid hunting alone.
- Learn to recognize bear sign, and avoid areas with fresh scat, diggings, tracks, or carcasses.
- Be cautious in dense timber or brush and along creeks and waterfalls.
- Always remain alert for sudden encounters.
- Carry EPA-registered bear spray. The recommended spray distance is twenty-five feet with a spray duration of a least six seconds.

Handling Your Game in the Field

- Keep bear spray readily available while handling game.
- Wear rubber gloves and an apron to minimize odors on clothing.
- Separate carcass from entrails, and remove carcass from area as soon as possible.
- Never leave entrails within one mile of a trail, campsite, picnic area, or parking lot.
- Make the carcass unavailable to bears by hanging it at least ten to fifteen feet from the ground and four feet out from the supporting structure. Also keep it a hundred yards away from any recreation site or sleeping areas.
- Hang the carcass where you can see it from a distance. That way you can observe it as you return to camp.

Food Regulations

- Keep human food and beverages, horse feeds, and dog food unavailable to bears unless it's being consumed, prepared for consumption, or transported.
- When departing an area, remove all food and refuse from any bear-resistant containers left in the area.
- Do not sleep in the same clothes in which you cooked or handled game.

- Keep sleeping bags, tents, and the sleeping area free of food and beverage odors.
- Always keep bear spray readily available.

KEEPING CHILDREN SAFE IN BEAR COUNTRY

Because children are the same size as some bears' natural prey, wild bears pose special dangers to all children. Parents should teach children that by protecting themselves they can protect bears.

- Children should always be within immediate sight and reach of adults.
- Children should be told not to play in or near dense brush.
- Children should avoid running along trails or areas with dense brush.
- Children should not make animal-like sounds while hiking or playing.
- Children should be warned not to approach bears, especially cubs.
- Children should never be encouraged to pet, feed, or pose for a photograph with bears in the wild, even if they appear tame.

BEAR SPRAY

Bear spray can play an important part in stopping bear attacks. It is an effective deterrent, but it can be adversely affected by wind, rain, and temperature. Make sure you purchase bear spray and not a personal

If everyone follows appropriate etiquette in bear country, there will be far fewer bear encounters. CUDDEBACK DIGITAL

...ense spray to protect yourself from bears. Although both types of sprays are made from Oleoresin Capsicum, capsaicin and related capsaicinoids are the active ingredients in bear spray.

The Environmental Protection Agency (EPA) regulates bear sprays. Look for the EPA registration and establishment numbers, usually found at the bottom of the front label. Only bear sprays will have labels that clearly refer to bears and state it is a bear deterrent or repellent or is to be used for stopping attacking bears.

Currently, the EPA requires that the concentration of Capsaicin and related capsaicinoids range between one and two percent. All will affect the eyes, nose, throat, and lungs of a bear. The variance in potency within the range is negligible.

Bear and wildlife management specialists, outfitters, guides, and individuals who have been involved in bear attacks recommend the following guidelines.

- Spray an amount containing at least 7.9 ounces or 225 grams for a minimum of six seconds. Try not to use all of the spray in one shot in case you are charged by more than one bear, charged more than once, or have more than one encounter.
- Spray from a distance of twenty-five feet to give the bear a chance to experience the effect of the spray and for it to become distracted and disabled from its charge.
- Point the canister toward the charging bear and slightly downward. If possible, spray before the bear is within twenty-five to thirty feet.
- Always keep the bear spray readily accessible. Remove the safety clip if you encounter fresh bear sign, if a bear is in the immediate area, and when you clean game or fish.
- Remember that bear spray is a good last line of defense, but it is not a substitute for vigilance and it does not replace appropriate safety techniques. Always try to leave the area or give the bear a chance to leave. Bear spray should only be used if you are charged by a bear.
- Do not use bear spray to harass or chase bears out of your yard. Call your local wildlife management agency to assist you.

In hopes of reducing the growing number of human/bear confrontations, the National Be Bear Aware and Wildlife Stewardship Campaign is dedicated to promoting safe and responsible stewardship of our wildlife treasures, especially bears. Since 1980, the Center for Wildlife Information has worked in partnership with state and federal wildlife and land management agencies. The educational concepts and materials have been tested in places such as Yellowstone National Park and Shoshone National Forest and through hunter education programs.

We can make a difference. Keeping people and bears safe is what it is all about. We must join together to preserve wild bears long into the future so that generations to come will have the opportunity to enjoy these majestic animals.

For more information, contact:
Center for Wildlife Information
P.O. Box 8289
Missoula, MT 59807
www.BeBearAware.org

CHAPTER 16

Favorite Hunts

Nothing is better than a good bear hunting story to get the juices flowing. And you just might learn something from the experience along the way. This radical bear hunter will share three of his all-time favorite bear hunting stories from his thirty-five-plus years pursuing these magnificent animals across North America.

A STEP BACK IN TIME

December howled outside my window as I sat in my game room, which doubles as my home office. The drudgery of paperwork never stood a chance, and as I glanced about the room my mind started to wander. The whistling wind began to evoke memories of past chases afield. My eyes settled on the St. Charles bows hanging on the wall, and a seed of a thought began to sprout in my fertile imagination. Wouldn't it be great to harvest a black bear with my takedown longbow made by the legendary St. Charles family? Perhaps the one signed and named "Yewphoria" for me by Glen himself.

Takedown longbows probably evolved as a result of the need for mid-nineteenth century gentlemen to take their bows in their carriages on the way to the archery range. Hence, the name "carriage bows." The St. Charles takedown longbow is a reproduction of the bow Glen built in 1942. My bow was built from a piece of yew wood that Glen had cut on Mount Rainier more than forty years ago and personally selected to fashion a bow for me.

The need for a longbow that easily can be carried in a quiver, or tucked into a compact car, or carried aboard an airplane (this may not be allowed today after 9-11) makes this bow an excellent choice for the traditional archer on the go. It is a precision instrument and then some, a thing of beauty shaped, sanded, and polished like a fine work of art. It is a piece of living history that has always been surrounded by romance and adventure.

As the plan took shape in my mind, I realized that I could add even more excitement to the hunt if I used an old arrow of Glen's that I had in my collection. This arrow sported an old Fred Bear broadhead. The arrow had been signed on the shaft by both Fred and Glen. Adding to the thrill of a bear hunt with this bow would be the possibility of losing or breaking this irreplaceable piece of memorabilia.

I already had a trip planned to Craig's Sporting Camp in New Brunswick, Canada—we were going north for spring bear and smallmouth bass fishing—and this seemed like the perfect place to try out my idea. The more I toyed with the notion, the more excited I got. I wanted to take a good representative of the black bear species, and I knew I would only get one chance at a shot, if one presented itself at all. In preparation for the hunt, I decided to make up a few practice arrows that would match the gram weight of Glen's old arrow. I certainly didn't want to take a chance of breaking his arrow during a practice session.

The winter months faded and spring was in high gear when the end of May arrived and it was finally time for my trip. With my friends Doug Sousa, vice president of OSEG (Outdoor Sports Expo Group), and Jim Kane, a professional tournament Bass fisherman, we loaded up the Suburban with the Champion boat in tow and headed north to New Brunswick. After about ten hours of driving, we arrived at camp on Saturday afternoon and were greeted by my friend Dale Craig, one of the owners of the lodge. We unloaded our gear in near ninety-degree temperatures and, work done, had dinner, swapping hunting stories with Dale and his brother Brian well into the night.

On Sunday, a nonhunting day in New Brunswick, we planned to take full advantage of the terrific smallmouth bass fishing on the St. John's River. The bear hunting would begin Monday afternoon, and Doug and I eagerly looked forward to hunting a bruin. Jim couldn't pull himself away from the water so he planned to do some serious fishing instead.

The temperature had dropped suddenly during the night, and it was about fifty degrees by Sunday morning, a lot more comfortable, to my way of thinking, for fishing and bear hunting. We loaded up our gear and headed to the river. The fish seemed sensitive to the quick change in temperature, and they weren't hitting as they should have. Still, we managed to catch close to one hundred fish, with a few nice ones over four pounds.

Monday dawned a bit warmer, but the fish still hadn't turned on yet. Doug and I quit fishing early to prepare for bear hunting. But by Monday evening, neither of us had taken nary a bear. I had seen a yearling bear at

While waiting for the bear hunt to resume, you can take advantage of some great fishing at many camps. Jim Kane removes bait before releasing this beauty.

my bait and watched it for a quarter of an hour or so but decided to pass on it. During the next couple of days, the fishing was better, but the hunting hadn't improved. I had seen another bear at my bait one evening close to dark, but since I didn't want to spook the bear from the bait, I decided to remain in my stand until it had left the area.

Friday evening came, and I started wondering if I would even get a shot at a bear. I arrived at my bait a bit early and began what is the arduous part of any hunt for me—the wait. The night was quite warm, and the bugs were out in full force, but my Bug Tamer outfit was doing its job of keeping the irritating insects off me. Time was dragging by, and I wasn't sure if that was good or bad. I realized that beyond trying my patience, the ticking clock meant I was fast losing any opportunity to see a bear.

No sooner had the thought popped into my mind when a bear appeared. He was moving out of the heavy cover about thirty yards to my right and was looking directly at my stand location. I froze. I even held my breath. That bruin stared at me for what must have been at least five minutes. He must have perceived no immediate threat because he then ambled toward the bait. But instead of stopping, he walked past it into heavy cover, circled behind the bait, and came out on the very path I had used to gain access to my stand. He took several more steps and looked up at me again.

I had a feeling that this bear had either been shot at before from this stand or been chased from the bait by a dominant boar in the past. He was extremely nervous about being at the bait area and was moving carefully and cautiously. He continued up the path to my stand, walking between me and the bait. Again I was under close scrutiny. I wasn't sure if I ever was going to get a chance for a shot. What was this fellow up to? All I could do was remain as still as possible and wait him out.

Suddenly he came straight for my tree. Almost instantly, he was within five feet of the tree, and I had visions of how quickly a black bear can climb a tree. I waited. After what seemed like an eternity, he turned away, heading to my right and the heavy cover he had originally left. As he turned and ever so slowly walked away, I realized that it was now or never. Here was the opportunity for which I had been waiting. When the bear reached the fifteen-yard line, I picked my spot, drew Yewphoria, and released Glen's old arrow with one smooth instinctive motion.

Its sound was magical music to my ears. This arrow that had seen such glorious experiences in its past was airborne once more. The thrill of the hunt had brought new life into this arrow as it took flight and found its mark.

I watched the tops of the cover sway back and forth as the bear bolted about fifty yards into heavy cover. I could hear it thrashing around for a few seconds, then all was still. I sat in my stand at least another thirty minutes to ensure that the bear had expired and that it was safe to approach him. As I waited, I recalled hearing Glen St. Charles, the founder of the Pope and Young Club, speaking at a Pope and Young convention many years ago. He talked about how many hunters today put too much emphasis upon trophy hunting. To him, a true trophy is measured by the time and effort the hunter puts into the hunt and the enjoyment and satisfaction he gleans from the experience.

I had just had one of the most thrilling experiences of my lifetime, and I somehow felt that Glen was with me in spirit. I descended the tree and located my bear, and as I neared I noticed that the arrow was still sticking out of the back and had not broken due to the angle of the shot. I felt Fred was with me as well. It seemed fitting that the arrow remained whole. Surely this arrow must have magical properties to have survived so many hunting experiences. By prevailing in one piece, it could live so

Dick Scorzafava with the bear he harvested with the nostalgic magic arrow and the bow named "Yewphoria."

that one day another hunter might hear its music and release its magic from the bow Yewphoria.

Since 1986 when this hunt took place, I have held Yewphoria in my hands many times and relived the wonderful memory of that experience.

LOADED FOR BEAR

Running hounds has been a special part of my life for many years. Although chasing bears with hounds has become controversial in recent years thanks to people who truly do not understand the thrill of the chase, such pursuits are steeped in tradition in our country. Listening to the sounds of the hounds in hot pursuit on a distant ridge or through a deep canyon is something all hunters should experience at least once in their lives. Nothing quite equals the lonely bawl or fast chop of a Plott or Treeing Walker hound, because that sound in itself is what this type of hunt is all about. It's the chase rather than the killing of the bear that really counts. After all, the good houndsmen that I know let more bears down the tree to run again another day.

Running hounds is an adventure that often leads you through some of the nastiest terrain imaginable and leaves miles of boot leather behind on the way to the treed bear. Any hunter who believes that hunting with hounds is easy has never been on a hound hunt in the mountains of the Northeast or Northwest.

The thrill of this hunt is why I got so excited when my friend Mike Mattly, the marketing director for Knight Rifles, called and asked me to set up a black bear hunt with hounds for him in the spring. Mike had never hunted black bear before, and this trip would be an opportunity for us to spend quality time together. Mike runs coyotes with hounds around his home in southern Iowa, and he wanted to try this method for hunting his first bear. For my part, I was looking forward to enjoying the chase with the hounds again while I could still get around the rugged places a bear usually leads us.

I contacted my friend Travis Reggear from north-central Idaho, who in my opinion is one of the best houndsmen in the country, to set up the trip. Travis is a "get 'er done" type of guy, and I knew he would go out of his way to find us some nice bears. The vast area that Travis hunts not only has a large number of bears, including some of the largest animals in the state, but it has a good road system that allows access to some really rugged country. Since you would need to be part mountain goat to get around in most of that area, the road system allows hunters more flexibility to get close enough to a treed bear and then hike in a reasonable distance.

On the first morning of our hunt, we had what appeared to be a 150-pound cinnamon sow treed by 8:30 A.M. Since this was the first morning, we decided that Mike should pass on this bear in the hopes that something better would emerge. We put leads on the hounds and slowly walked away, turning after a distance to watch the bear zip down the tree like a fireman down a pole. Within seconds, the bear had disappeared like a ghost into the thick forest.

Not quite an hour had passed until we had a second chase going. When we arrived at the tree, Travis and I decided to recommend that Mike also pass on this animal, a beautiful glossy black bear that appeared to be a little larger than the first bear. By looking at the head shape, the width of the front pads, and the overall body length, we determined it was another dry sow. After taking pictures, we put leads on the hounds again and led them away from the tree. When we were far enough away, we turned, sat on the ground quickly, and watched the bear come down the tree and scramble off. One of the things I like about hunting bears with hounds is that you have time to evaluate the animals. Most good

The 150-pound cinnamon bear treed by 8:30 A.M. the first day of the hunt.

houndsmen I've known over the years let many more bears down the tree to run again another day than they actually harvest. It's the thrill of the chase that counts, and once the bear is treed the dogs have won.

We actually had two bears up a tree by 11:30 A.M. on the first day, something I have only seen happen twice in all the years I have been pursuing black bear. Mike was having a ball watching and listening to the hounds. It takes hounds with speed and grit to tree a bear. Since many bears do not like to tree, they first have to be caught. All the hounds in the pack must be in the race, and they all have to be at the tree. It's difficult to breed grit, speed, and brains all together in a hound, but Travis and his friend Mike Kemp from Three Bears Kennels have developed a great strain of hounds. They are the best handling and fastest treeing dogs I have seen in almost forty years. They can strike a bear on a rig in the air from a long way off and know exactly where the track is when they hit the ground, a sense few hounds ever develop. I've seen many dogs over the years strike off the rig, go the wrong way, and have to take several minutes to straighten out the tracks before lining out in the right direction on the bear tracks. Not Travis's hounds. When they strike, you better start cutting other dogs into them quickly, or you will have the hounds strung out across the countryside.

If dogs can handle the dense cover and mountainous terrain of north-central Idaho, they will be able to run a bear anywhere across the North American range. On the way back to the house, I told Mike that these dogs were spoiling him. Normally if hounds can tree one or two bears on an entire trip, it would be considered a successful hunt. He had heard the chase and witnessed two bears treed before noon on the first day.

The next morning we were out early, rigging the mountains with ATVs when suddenly the hounds struck hard off the rig. We all scrambled to cut the hounds, and the race was on. We ran to the top of the hill and listened to the hound music echo through the canyon as the dogs pushed the bear over the top of the next mountain and out of earshot. The race was going on for almost two hours when we began to realize this must be a big bear. We could tell by listening to the hounds that he had been baying up on the ground and chasing the dogs. They would be hot on the trail using their high-pitched bawl and chop voices when the noise would suddenly stop, indicating that the chase was turned around and the bear was chasing them. Since the day was warming up, we decided to get as close to the chase as possible and turn in another pack of six or eight fresh hounds in the hopes of pushing this old bear up a tree.

Another three hours went by and the chase was still on. This bear refused to tree. He was still baying up, chasing, and fighting the hounds. We had to do something fast or some of the hounds were going to get seriously hurt. Our group decided that Mike and Travis would get ahead of the chase and try to head them off so that Mike could shoot the bear on the ground. We would make our way around to the chase and release the balance of the hounds to put as much pressure on the bear as possible.

After seven hours into the chase, Mike finally was able to put a hole in the bear with his Knight Vision muzzleloader as the animal crossed an old logging road. Mike made a perfect split-second shot, and the bear folded up within a few feet. The chase was finally over, and Mike had an old boar that measured 6 feet 6 inches nose to tail, with a beautiful coal black hide and a skull that would surely make the Longhunters Society record book. He also got to experience what it's like when a bear does not want to tree. This old brute would have never treed no matter how many hounds we put on him. I have never seen a bear that would not tree with that much hound power at his tail.

In just a few days of hunting, Mike learned what it was like to put a daypack on his back, sling his Knight muzzleloader over his shoulder, and trek across the steep mountains and canyons of Idaho in the heat of

Mike and Travis with a group of the hounds that aided Mike on his first bear hunt. And what a bear he harvested!

the day in pursuit of a pack of hounds, hightailing it after a mean old monster bear. To make the trek even more demanding, we were pelted with intermittent heavy downpours. Mike really earned his trophy on this trip, and I was happy to have been there to share the experience with him. Since we were able to capture most of the hunt on film for a television show, Mike will be able to relive the thrill of his hunt again and again.

We took the next day off to give the hounds (and ourselves) a much-needed rest. But the next morning, we awoke refreshed and ready to go again. Today was my opportunity for an Idaho bear behind hounds. I was content to be in this beautiful country creating memories with close friends, but I knew an opportunity at a good bear would be the icing on the cake.

The morning started out slowly as we rigged the hounds through the rugged country. Then as we turned a corner, the hounds struck hard on a bear and ran up the mountain creating loud music to our ears before advancing farther and farther out of hearing range. We jumped on our ATVs and raced up the mountain to listen to the chase and get a handle on which direction they were going. In the distance, we could hear them faintly, and it sounded as though they had the bear treed already. We moved to a better position to listen and sure enough the bear was in a tree while the hounds hammered away at it.

I loaded up my backpack full of cameras and slung my Knight Revolution over my shoulder as we set off on foot to follow the hound music to the tree. The closer we got to the tree, the louder the hound music became. At the tree the noise was so deafening, we had to actually talk into each other's ears. The sounds of the hounds' voices were magnified by the deep canyon we were in and the stillness of the morning.

Travis and I smiled at each other once we evaluated the bear his hounds had treed. It was a little black-colored bear, probably two or three years old and about 100 pounds. Everyone rounded up the hounds onto leads, took a few pictures, and walked away so the bear would come down the tree. I love to watch a bear come down a tree and virtually vanish into the forest in a few short seconds. There one second, gone the next.

By the time we all got back to the rigs, it was starting to get late so we called it a day. We planned to get an early start in the morning on what would be my last day to hunt. Travis told me they were going to rig three packs of hounds in hopes of getting a good bear chase going early. Mike Kemp's and Mike Stockton's hounds would be the other packs rigging the countryside, and if they struck a bear, they would look for sign to determine the size of the bear. If it looked promising, they would radio us so we could hurry to the location before releasing our hounds.

We had been rigging about an hour when Mike Stockton called on the radio to tell us his dogs had struck hard off the rig. He had examined the area for sign and found a large track in the sand on the shoulder of an old logging road. Mike yelled over the radio to get over there quickly because he was sure this was the bear we were after. He also told us he was going to release his three dogs. When we arrived at the location, the race was on and the hounds were completely out of hearing. We had to use their telemetry units to get a location on them.

They were over the top of the next mountain heading straight away from us, so we fired up our ATVs and raced up the road over the mountain. After cresting the top, we all stopped to listen, and it sounded like the bear was already treed. We tried to get as close as possible, then loaded up our gear, and headed into the tree. When we were within a hundred yards of the tree, the bear bailed out of the tree. We just didn't have enough dog power to keep him up and he must have heard us coming. Rushing back to the rigs, we decided to try heading off the race and cutting Mike Kemp's pack into the other three hounds that were chasing the bear.

Everything went as planned. We now had a total of nine hounds in the race, and we all hoped it would be enough to keep the bear treed the next time. We weren't looking forward to another strenuous all-day hunt on the ground chasing the bear through some of the thickest, steepest, and roughest country one could imagine. Many places the terrain is so steep you would have to be part mountain goat just to navigate through it.

The race went on for another two hours, and we actually watched and listened from on top of a mountain for almost half an hour as the hounds pushed the bear through a canyon. We saw the bear twice as he crossed logging roads. As the hound music echoed off the canyon walls, it was like sitting in a seat at a concert with the spectacular Idaho Mountains as the backdrop. The concert paused when the race crested over the mountain in front of us. We all ran to our machines and ripped through the canyon and over the mountain so we could get close to the race again. And just as we came over the top of the mountain, we could hear the grand finale to the concert. The hounds had the bear treed about halfway down the valley. We scrambled to get our gear and rushed down to the tree as quietly as possible to ensure that the bear would not bail out again.

We found the old bear way up at the top of a thick pine tree. The tree was so thick that I had a hard time seeing the bear. Everyone ran around tying back dogs while I tried to determine where to take my shot from. I decided that the best shot was going to be directly from the base of the tree straight up through all the branches. I hoped it would take out his front shoulders and exit out of the neck.

Taking careful aim and bracing myself against the tree, I slowly squeezed the trigger until my Knight Revolution shattered the sound of the canine orchestra. With shaking hands, I dropped three Triple Seven pellets down the pipe, followed by a 290-grain polymer tip boat tail bullet, and then concentrated on dropping a disc into the muzzleloader to finish my reload. Suddenly, I heard a branch snap, and everyone was yelling at me to get out of there because the bear was coming out. I ran quickly away from the tree to avoid the bear landing on me.

He hit the ground and never moved a muscle. A beautiful animal measuring 6 feet 5 inches nose to tail, he had an extremely thick black robe and a big pumpkin head. I was totally ecstatic about this hunt. The actual shooting of the bear itself was nothing more than a closing episode in a journey that that left miles of footprints across some of the most rugged country imaginable.

Scorzafava with his Idaho trophy, taken with the help of his friend Travis Reggear and Travis's hounds.

I knew from years of experience that the bear had more than enough bone on his skull to stretch the tape to more than 19 inches for the record book, but keeping score does not strike much of an interest in me. This bear made *my* book, and that's what really counts. As I measured him, I knew I would not get the animal officially measured. This hunt was far too special to me for that. Creating memories with good friends in special places while listening to the concert of the hounds' music echo through a deep canyon from the top of a mountain is as close to heaven as it gets here on earth.

IN SEARCH OF BIGFOOT IN THE LAND OF GIANTS

I've been chasing big bears around North America for most of my life and have had the good fortune to put my tag on a few big bruisers over the years, so the mission on this northern adventure was to harvest a true monster bear for my dad. His health had been failing for the last few months, and I was going to cancel this trip, but he knew how excited I was about hunting this virgin spot, so he told me to go and kill him a big bear.

The area I would be hunting in northern Manitoba hadn't been bear hunted for the last several years, yet the outfitters had been baiting the area for the last two years to establish the baits. It was the type of location that true trophy bear hunters dream about—isolated and almost untouched by humans. Spring in northern Manitoba is when the bears emerge from hibernation and the birds return from their southern journey. The forest explodes with life as the countryside seems to come alive. It's the perfect time of year for nature lovers, fishermen, and—of course—radical bear hunters to be in the outdoors.

This rugged wilderness is home to abundant black bears and some of the best northern pike fishing in North America. When the plane starts to descend into the Lynn Lake Airport, there's no mistaking that this is Canada's true north—strong, free, rugged, silent, and majestic. This is the Land of Little Sticks where even the trees sometimes seem to be struggling against the harsh elements of nature. The enchanting beauty from the call of a loon across a tranquil lake on a cool spring night will take away all your stresses. Ecologically significant eskers made of gravel from the remnants of glaciers from centuries ago serve as proof of the forces of nature. Up here in the transition between the boreal forest and the northern tundra, no ringing phones will distract you and no traffic jams will keep you from where you're going. At night, you have a perfect view of the canopy of stars overhead.

Located at the end of Provincial Highway #391, the community of Lynn Lake was carved out of the northern Manitoba wilderness to serve a nickel mine. The history of the town is unique and fascinating. Lynn Lake was a mining community built in the early 1950s from homes moved, over lake ice and winter roads, from a place called Sherridon 150 miles south. With over fifty portages, the trail passed over frozen muskeg and lakes and went through bush and ravines. Because of the terrain, the road was only useable between freeze-up and spring thaw. At other times of the year, the land overflowed with water, causing anything crossing it to sink deep into the muskeg and become rendered unable to move. All the mines have closed down now, and there are just over five hundred residents in the community at this time.

I arrived at my final destination in a single-engine Beaver with floats. Golden Eagle Lodge, one of those places that make up the final frontier of Canadian bear hunting, is located on Sickle Lake, approximately forty air miles from the town of Lynn Lake. The main lodge overlooks beautiful, unspoiled Sickle Lake, and that made me want to grab my fly rod and wet a fly right away. Lodge manager Jason Dyck greeted us as we exited the float plane. Jason and I seemed to hit it off right from the start as we swapped bear stories we had experienced. He reminded me of myself when I was young: all business and dedicated to producing results for clients. Golden Eagle runs a small operation that prides itself on quality rather than quantity when it comes to bear hunting and fishing. There is a vast amount of land to hunt on, but the operation only accommodates a few hunters each year to ensure that quality trophy bears are taken every spring. As a matter of fact, I was the second and last hunter for the year. The first hunter was a woman bowhunter who passed on several animals before killing a bear that almost stretched the tape to 7 feet nose to tail on her third day.

Sickle Lake is fifteen and one-half miles long, and Jason suggested I stay at the Keewatin Point Outpost Post Camp near the mouth of the Keewatin River to save transportation time back and forth from the lodge at the extreme other end of the lake. He had a number of established baits in the area and had seen the sign that a real monster was coming into one of them. Jason suggested I spend the morning looking at the baits with him, and we could then determine which ones to hunt.

Every one of the six baits we examined had been hit, but there were two baits in tight dark locations less than two hundred yards from the lake's edge we both really liked. We decided to hunt the one that would give the best wind direction to the bait from the treestand each day. I had a good feeling about these baits. They just looked like big bear spots, places where the bears would feel comfortable moving in and out of during daylight hours.

To the inexperienced, hunting spring black bear over bait might not appear gratifying or fair, but believe me, it is a tremendous experience. Any bear that is baited is not a pushover, and this is especially true of the trophy bruins over seven years old. They hit baits infrequently, many times well after legal hunting hours are past. These big guys always circle a bait to check the wind and to ease in with all their senses revved to the limit. Wise old boars are anything but simple to get a shot at.

I'd been sitting in my treestand for more than five hours on the first night without seeing a thing. I had been thinking about my dad and praying I would be able to come through for him with the big bear he asked me to get, when seemingly out of nowhere a snowshoe hare and her brood of young appeared. They started feeding around the bait, and instantly I thought what a place for a bunch of hare to hang out and have a bite to eat. If a bear came into the bait, they could become the meal. They were still feeding at the end of shooting light, and since a bear never showed, I climbed out of my stand and walked to the pickup point.

The next two evenings on the stand were quiet with no activity. As I sat, my mind kept reflecting back to past fishing and hunting trips I took as a kid with my dad. Several times I had to hold back tears because I knew this special person in my life wouldn't be with me much longer, and I was having difficulty dealing with that fact. I also started to realize this was day three of my trip, and I hadn't seen any movement at the baits. Jason had told me this evening on the way into the bait that the other baits had not been hit either for the last three days. Something was wrong.

I have seen this happen before in other places in the spring of the year. Usually it means that a favorite natural food source has become available, and the bears will shut down on the baits for a week or so before returning. I knew this could be a major problem because I only had three days remaining on this hunt. Jason and I would have to put our heads together and develop a plan for the balance of the hunt to try and ensure opportunity, if not success.

We discussed the situation on the way back to camp and decided to put a couple Cuddeback digital scouting cameras on each of the two baits that night. We also agreed that the bears must be feeding on some natural food source since they were not visiting the baits. We decided to hang a new beaver carcass high in the air at the baits in the hopes that a bear would wind the odor and come into the baits again.

The next evening found me in the stand once again waiting for something to happen, when suddenly I heard something behind me. I slowly turned my head to catch a glimpse of the pumpkin-sized head of a monster bear slowly circling behind the bait. He never came into the bait, and I only had about twenty minutes remaining of shooting light. On the trail to the left of the bait, I caught some movement out of the corner of my eye and saw a large black timber wolf sneaking into the opening of the bait area. As he entered, he gazed around and stopped to look directly at me in the stand. He stared at me with his bluish-green eyes, and I had an eerie feeling as though he were looking right through me. Then he suddenly walked past the bait opening and disappeared behind the bait. By now shooting light was over, and I knew I had to descend my stand soon to meet Jason at the pickup point. I was wondering where the wolf had gone in the darkness of the night when I heard Jason arrive with the boat. I carefully got out of the stand and briskly walked on the path to the pickup point, with an arrow nocked on my Mathews rest for reassurance. Excited about the event, I immediately told Jason my story of the evening's happenings.

Time was counting down, and we only had two days of hunting remaining for me to get that big bear. On the next afternoon, the wind really picked up and began swirling in several directions like a front was coming through the area. When it was time to go out to the stand for the evening hunt, the wind was actually howling and it had just begun to spit rain. Jason and I shook our heads in disappointment. We both knew from experience the bears would not move much in that kind of wind. On top of that, the wind was coming off the lake and it would be blowing across my back, taking my scent into the baits. Disappointed but resigned to let the baits sit for the evening, I decided to try some pike fishing.

After loading our gear in the boat, we started fishing, trying different lures and flies to entice a big northern to strike. We slowly worked our way around the lake, trying to locate the fish and catching a few fish but nothing of size. Finally, I got a hard hit and could tell instantly from the tug that this was a good fish burning line off my Abel reel. The back-and-forth battle of the fish taking line and me retrieving it lasted almost twenty minutes before I was able to get him on the side of the boat and into a net. But just as Jason touched the net on the water, the big fish rolled making a big splash. Under and around the boat it swam several times until finally we got him into the net. What a fish! Jason realized by sight that he might be a contender for a Manitoba Master Angler Award. We measured him, and sure enough he was 41 inches, the minimum required for the award. After taking a few quick pictures, we released the

Dick with the 41-inch northern pike.

fish back into the cold water. I yelled out, "Dad, that was for you!" as he swam away.

Almost immediately, I had another good hit, this time a nice 37-inch fish, then another 39-inch, a few 35- and 36-inchers before finally hooking the monster of the day, a 43-incher. We had found the fish and made the proper presentation to them for a strike. When all was said and done, in about an hour and a half we caught nine fish over 36 inches long, two of which were Master Angler fish, and that is unheard of anywhere. I'd go back to Golden Eagle Lodge just to have the opportunity to fish Sickle Lake again.

It was time to pick up and get moving as daylight was fading quickly. On the way back as we came around a point not far from the bait, a black blob appeared in the lake about two hundred yards to my left. I pointed it out to Jason, and we decided to go take a look. As we approached with the boat, we were surprised to see a mature bear swimming across the lake from the back side of the bait. We pulled in front of him with the boat and noticed his head was cut up and bloody. He also had no intention of turning back in the direction from which he had come. He was swimming across that lake, and he didn't care what was in front of him!

I have come across many animals swimming lakes or rivers over my years, and every time you go in front of them with the boat, they turn back in the direction they came because they feel it's safer. We figured that this guy just had his butt kicked by a monster boar and was not going back for more. He was getting out of the big bear's way, no matter what. The big old bear must have been laid up close to the bait when this guy came in and all hell broke lose. Many times an old boar will take possession of a feed source and will chase away anything that comes into his space. This made my day because I knew the boar was back, and maybe we would finally get to see him on my last day.

On the way to the bait from camp, Jason and I discussed a plan for the last evening's hunt. We would go in a few hours earlier than we had been hunting, and I would quickly get settled in the stand while Jason quietly baited the two barrels. Then he would softly tap the barrels with a stick to give the illusion of something feeding at the bait before rushing to the boat and exiting the area. He would also leave an orange vest next to the shore of the pickup point, and if I did get a shot I was to hang the vest so he could come back from the other side of the lake where he planned to fish.

Everything went as planned, and Jason gave me the thumbs-up before exiting to the boat. It was extremely quiet, and I could hear him get in the boat, start the motor, and speed across the lake. Now the wait began. I looked into the crystal-clear sky and prayed for God's help on this, the last night of my hunt, before picking up my Mathews bow and nocking an arrow. The sit began. I've gotten better at sitting and waiting over the years as I have matured, but it's still difficult to sit still for hours on end.

I had been sitting motionless and scent-free in my treestand for just under an hour waiting patiently for Old Bigfoot, as I had named him, to show at the bait when from the corner of my eye I sensed some type of movement. Ever so slowly, I turned my head, and there he stood just behind my stand on my right, appearing like a phantom out of thin air. I gulped . . . and then relaxed.

He looked bigger than a Volkswagen when he stepped from behind my stand at approximately twenty yards. His head was enormous, wide with bulging mounds on both sides and a deep crease down the top. The ears looked small, his belly hung low, and he was exceptionally long in length. He had an extremely thick dense shiny coat, so thick you could see it split when he moved. I could actually see it glistening in the setting sun. His body was frozen in place as he swiveled his heavy head, sniffing the air. Then suddenly he shuffled slowly and cautiously closer to the bait and into my bow range. I coaxed him forward in my mind—"Only about five more steps, big boy. Come on now, keep coming."—as my fingers curled tighter around my release.

I could tell by his body language he had no clue I was waiting in ambush. If these big old boars sense something is wrong or if they slightly catch wind of your human scent, they will not come into the bait until well after dark, if at all. A black bear has a much better sense of smell than even a white-tailed deer, and I had done all the normal precautions of keeping my scent under control by showering and spraying my equipment with Scent Killer spray, wearing Scent-Lok BaseSlayers under my Scent-Lok jacket and pants, and sporting a head cover and gloves.

The bear passed in front of the two barrels, causing them to completely disappear from view. I sucked in a deep breath as in an instant he was in a quartering-away position with his huge front leg stretched out and presenting what I had been waiting for—the perfect shot opportunity. Now it was up to me. I slowly drew my Mathews to full draw, anchored, put my Black Gold fiber optic sight pin on the spot, and sent my Carbon Express arrow sizzling through the air. Almost instantly, I heard the impact of the hit and watched the orange Blazer vanes vanish. He literally dropped in his tracks and piled up in a big heap. The Rage broadhead had severed his spinal cord and skewered both heart and lungs for an instant kill.

I shot up on the platform of my stand, raised my arms in the air, and screamed a victorious "YES! Thank you, dear Lord. Dad, this was for you!" before sitting back down and waiting for my thundering pulse to return to normal. Encountering this gargantuan bear did not happen by chance. As I marveled at the bear's size from my perch, I was thinking of what I have stressed to the many people who attend my seminars each year at the sportsmen shows.

I learned a long time ago that if you want to kill big bears, you have to hunt where big bears exist, and those places are getting more difficult to locate. Not all areas are created equal when it comes to big-game animals, especially record book class black bears. A study of the Pope and Young or Boone and Crockett record books will confirm that fact. I truly believe it's harder to kill a big black bear that will qualify for record book entry today than it is to kill a big white-tailed deer.

Dick with the giant bigfoot bear.

It's even getting much harder to find a truly big black bear of trophy class in the remote locations of North America. I know the real key to growing big bears is age. Boars that exceed 500 pounds are between seven and fifteen years old. When I chose this remote location of Manitoba, I knew it was virtually the end of the road in the northwestern section of that Canadian province on the edge of the Boreal Forest. The bears in this vast country receive very little hunting pressure at all. Certainly the big black bears that I target are extraordinary for their size. They rival and even exceed a grizzly bear in stature.

Jason and I spent many minutes admiring the size and beauty of this behemoth of a bear, everything from his battle-scarred head to his thick fur and gigantic front pads that measured over 7 inches across. His hide measured 7 feet 8 inches nose to tail. We estimated from measurements that he was between 550 and 600 pounds, huge for a spring bear. The skull green scored a whopping $22^2/_{16}$ inches, and he had a neck measurement of 33 inches. From the wear on his teeth, we guessed he was at least fifteen years old. He will be my finest black bear ever, and he is dedicated to my dad. Just knowing he has more kin in the area will be enough to bring me back to the land of giants in search of another bigfoot.

I called my dad as soon as I arrived in Winnipeg on June 12 to tell him the whole story of the monster bear I had killed for him. He was happy and told me he was proud of me and loved me, but I could tell from his voice his health was failing even more since I had begun the trip. My dad passed away on June 13, 2006, about two hours after I got home from this trip. I think he was waiting to say his good-byes.

CHAPTER 17

Radically Close Calls

Bears can be dangerous animals, whether you are a researcher, a hunter, or a guide. Be around them long enough, and you'll eventually get close enough to smell a black bear's putrid breath. This radical bear hunter wants to share some of his close encounters with bruins and teach you a bit about bear hunting safety in the process.

RIGHT IN MY FACE

Back many years ago when I was young and running bear hounds with a friend of mine three or four times a week just for the excitement of the chase, our state bear biologist called and asked if we would be interested in helping him tag and telemetry collar a few black bears. He wanted to monitor the species to determine the size of their home ranges and where they den for the winter. If we were able to collar a few females, the biologists could go to their dens every winter to change their collars, weigh them, and check their overall health. If they had cubs, the biologists could check the health of them, too, while also tagging and collaring them.

We jumped at what we saw as another opportunity to run our hounds and do something to protect the future of the bears in our home state of Massachusetts.

On three occasions, we went out and treed three different bears for him. The biologist was especially pleased because two of the bears were mature sows. The other was a nice boar that weighed in at 255 pounds in August. As a side note, we weighed that same bear in January after he bulked up for the winter hibernation, and he weighed 365 pounds. He was as fat as a pig and in great physical condition.

On our fourth outing, we treed a bear early in the morning. The bear was rather high in an old, thick, pine tree where the branches made it difficult to get a shot at the animal from the ground. I decided to climb up the tree for a clearer shot with the tranquilizer gun. I hit the bear in the rump, and she started to fall out of the tree through some branches in my direction. Luckily for me, she was stopped by a couple huge branches about five feet above my head as I was frantically trying to get down and out of her way.

We ended up spending a lot of time getting the bear out of the tree using a couple ropes and a strap, so it wouldn't get injured falling to the ground. Next, we began to work on the bear, putting in an ear tag and a telemetry collar, weighing the bear, and checking its vitals. I was kneeling down next to the bear holding her rear leg up so that the biologist could give her an injection in the rump, when suddenly she sat up, opened her mouth wide in my face, and made a deep growling sound. Then she hit me in the shoulder with her front pad. I rolled over, got up, and started running before one of my friends hit her right in the nose with a walking stick he was holding. She changed direction and ran off into the woods.

That close encounter really shook me up. She was about six inches from my face when she opened her mouth, and I will never forget the smell of her putrid breath. Any one of us could have been severely injured or even killed by that bear, even though she only weighed 130 pounds. I gained a lot more respect for black bears that day, and we all learned some important lessons. After that experience, before working on a bear we always tied the front and rear legs together and put duct tape around its muzzle. We also made sure someone was standing nearby with the tranquilizer gun ready to tranquilize the bear again in case it awoke before we were finished.

IN THE TREESTAND

On the first night of a hunt to Saskatchewan, I was sitting over bait with only my bow and six arrows. It was a clear, quiet night, and I had been on my stand for approximately three hours when all of a sudden a bear came into the area from behind the bait. It looked like an immature male about three or four years old. He stayed at the bait for almost thirty minutes munching down the goodies before putting his nose in the air to smell something from the direction of my treestand. Then he walked briskly to my tree and started smelling the tree. As I looked down through the grate of my treestand, I could see the bear actually licking the tree and the tree steps I used to climb up into my stand. Incredibly, he started to climb the tree to my position! When he reached the base of my treestand, I yelled at him loudly, "Hey, bear, get out of here!" I really don't know who was more surprised at this point—him or me. He did not react as most bears would by backing down the tree and running off. Instead, he started to

The infamous treestand bear, on the way to Dick's tree.

push his head up against the underside of my treestand, which made the base of my stand rise up before actually dropping about an inch. At this point I realized I had to do something quickly or this bear could possibly knock me right out of the stand. I started screaming at him and jumping on the base of the stand in an attempt to get him to back off and go down the tree. He reacted by getting more aggressive and trying to swat at my leg with his front paw. This guy was not going to back off, and I knew I had to do something quickly or I was going to be in deep trouble. I grabbed the arrow off my quiver, held onto the tree with one arm, leaned over as far as I could, and jabbed him straight down on the tip of his nose. He started bleeding like a stuck pig and immediately backed down the tree and ran off into the forest. I began to shake all over and had to sit down in the seat of my stand for a few minutes to regain my composure.

I didn't see another bear for the remainder of the evening, and when the guide came in to pick me up at dark I told him the story and showed him the blood all over the tree. He told me that this must have been the same bear that chased him off the bait one afternoon when he was baiting the barrel and he had to shoot into the air to get him to back off.

We later found out that one of his young guides had replenished the bait barrel early that afternoon and when he had finished had put up my treestand. He put in my tree steps and hung the stand wearing the same gloves he used to put the meat scraps in the barrel at the bait. The bear smelled this and probably thought that something good to eat was up in the tree. He must have been surprised to find me sitting there and responded with aggression. You think *he* was surprised?

I did not hunt that bait site again while I was at camp, but I ended up shooting a nice cinnamon bear two days later from a scent-free stand. From that day on, every time I go on a hunt I always ask the guide when the stand was put up in the tree and who put it up. I then ask if they used gloves and if they baited the barrel with the same gloves. Knowing this ensures my safety and the safety of anyone else in camp.

THE KNOCKOUT

I observed another bear encounter while on a hound hunt in the northeast kingdom of Vermont with a group of friends in the late 1970s. The dogs lined out on a bear that took off straight out of the country for miles. It was one of these immature bears that likes to run, and this bear took us on a merry chase for several hours before, for some reason, it started to bay up on the ground. We saw the bear cross an old logging road, and after deciding it was 125 pounds and not worth the chase we tried to round up the hounds. By driving around the old logging roads and listening to the chase, we attempted to get ahead of the chase several times to pull the hounds off the bear.

We finally were able to get between the bear and the hounds to pick up a few of the dogs, but we still had three hounds on the ground in hot pursuit. We rode around for about another hour until we found a location where we could hear the chase again. The three hounds had the bear bayed up in a thick swamp, so we decided to run in and try to call them off the bear. The closer we got to them, the louder the hound music echoed out of the swamp and the hounds could not hear us calling. When we reached the area, we saw the bear sitting down in the water using its front paws to hook any dog that came near. The hounds would not respond to our calling so we knew we had to get close and put leads on the dogs.

We decided to approach the bear from behind in hopes that the hounds would come to us as we got closer. We all moved in slowly in a straight line at the bear. When we got to within twenty yards of the bear, all the dogs came to us and we were able to grab two of them by the collar. But the other dog ran around behind the bear and bit it on the butt, causing the bear to chase it. We all started yelling at the bear so it wouldn't notice one of our buddies circling the bear to get the dog. As my friend bent down to grab the dog by the collar, he wasn't watching the bear, and it swatted him on the side of his face with a front paw. The impact knocked him completely off his feet, and he fell onto the floor of the swamp, out cold. The bear then turned and ran off into the woods while one of the other members of our group was able to grab the last dog.

We all rushed over to our friend to determine the extent of his injuries. It took a couple minutes before he regained consciousness. He was lucky the bear only hit him with the base of its pad rather than its claws because with the force he was hit it would have ripped his face apart. As it was, his face was bruised and starting to swell so we got him up and off to the hospital to be checked by a doctor.

After some X-rays to check his eye and ear, the doctors determined he was just badly bruised and that he would be sore for the next few days and would need quiet and plenty of rest.

I will never forget how he looked the day after his encounter with the bear. His face was so swollen and black and blue that he didn't look like the same person. One eye was completely closed, his nose was twice its normal size, and his ear was swollen and red as a tomato. It took him almost two weeks to recover from his injuries, but the psychological damage never went away. Over the years whenever he hunted with us and we had a bear bayed on the ground by the hounds, he would never come in with us even if we were going to shoot the bear on the ground. He wanted nothing to do with any bear on the ground. One close encounter was enough for him.

THE FIRST AND LAST BEAR HUNT

Several years ago, I was guiding a woman on her first hunt for black bear in Canada. She had hunted white-tailed deer and turkey before but had never before seen a live black bear, even in a zoo. After meeting her in camp and seeing how nervous she was about this hunt, I asked if she wanted me to sit with her for the first few nights on the stand. She quickly accepted my offer. A lot of people had filled her mind with scary bear stories and told her she would be lucky if she came home alive.

The first night, we were in separate treestands with bases almost touching so I could calm her down and communicate if a bear was at the bait. We were on stand for a few hours when suddenly a bear came into the opening from our right. When she saw the bear coming to our stand location, her eyes grew to the size of golf balls, but she didn't move or make a peep. The bear stopped and stared at us in the stand for a few seconds before proceeding to the bait. When he reached the bait, she slowly turned her head to me and whispered, "Oh my God, is it ever beautiful."

We watched the bear for several minutes and waited for it to move into a position for a good killing shot. When finally it stood broadside, I gave her a quick nod to indicate that she should take the shot and she slowly raised her gun, took careful aim, and squeezed the trigger. She hit that bear hard, and it literally did a back flip before running into the thick dense swamp to the left of the bait.

I told her it looked like a good shot and that we should wait a few minutes before I went down to find him. Light was fading quickly. Taking my gun, I climbed down the tree and told her to stay there until I could check out the situation. I walked over to where the bear had entered the swamp and saw a very visible blood trail. Slowly and quietly, I followed the blood into the swamp when suddenly I heard her start yelling, "Where are you, Dick?" I didn't answer, and in another few seconds, she called again, this time louder, "Where are you? I can't see you." Again I didn't answer. I didn't want to let the bear know where I was if he was still alive, but she must have been nervous when I didn't answer her calls.

Unexpectedly, I heard something in front of me and stopped in my tracks to listen. Suddenly less than ten feet away, the bear stood up on its hind legs and stared directly at me. Instantly and without hesitation, I raised my gun and shot him in the throat. He immediately fell to the ground dead. I returned to the stand and helped my client down the tree. She was upset but glad to see that I was safe. I was a little edgy myself from the experience but tried to hold my emotions inside so she would calm down. After a few minutes of talking, she was fine and I took her over to see her trophy bear. She told me this was her first and last bear hunt because she now realized that these animals can really hurt a person.

These are just a few of my experiences with close encounters over the years. I probably could write an entire book about my hunting experiences alone. With the stories I told here, this radical bear hunter just wanted to make sure you understand that the black bear is a wild animal and can become aggressive at anytime. The black bear is a majestic, exciting animal to hunt, but it also can be extremely dangerous. Please be safe and careful in the bear woods.

Resources

Alpen Optics
10329 Dorset Street
Rancho Cucamonga, CA 91730
919-987-8370
www.alpenoptics.com

**Black Gold Premium Bowsights
and Free Fall Rests**
25-B Shawnee Way
Bozeman, MT 59715
406-586-1117
www.montanablackgold.com

Bohning Company, Ltd.
7361 North Seven Mile Road
Lake City, MI 49651
231-229-4247
www.bohning.com

Carbon Express Arrows
P.O. Box 380
Flushing, MI 48433
810-733-6360
www.carbonexpressarrows.com

Cuddeback Digital Scouting Cameras
DeerCam
Non-Typical, Inc.
860 Park Lane
Park Falls, WI 54552
715-762-2260
www.cuddebackdigital.com

Double Bull Archery LLC
301 County Road 43
Big Lake, MN 55309
888-464-0409
www.doublebullarchery.com

Field Logic, Inc
The Block 4X4
101 Main Street
Superior, WI 54880
715-395-9955
www.fieldlogic.com

Gamehide Hunting Wear
CORE Resources,Inc.
1503 East Highway 13
Burnsville, MN 55337
888-267-3591
www.gamehide.com

Heat Factory
2390 Oak Ridge Way
Vista, CA 92083
800-993-4328
www.heatfactory.com

Knight Rifles
715B Summit Drive SW
Decatur, AL 35601
541-856-2626
www.knightrifles.com

Mathews, Inc.
919 River Road
P.O. Box 367
Sparta, WI 54656
608-269-2728
www.mathewsinc.com

Rage Broadhead
101 Main Street
Superior, WI 54880
715-395-0020
www.ragebroadheads.com

Rivers Edge Treestands
Ardisam, Inc.
1360 First Avenue
P.O. Box 666
Cumberland, WI 54829
800-345-6007
www.ardisam.com

Scent-Lok Technologies
1731 Wierengo Drive
Muskegon, MI 49442
800-315-5799
www.scentlok.com

Wildlife Research Center
1050 McKinley Street
Anoka, MN 55303
800-873-5873
www.wildlife.com

Zebra Strings
919 River Road
P.O. Box 367
Sparta, WI 54656
608-269-1235
www.zebrastrings.com

Thorlos
2210 Newton Drive
Statesville, NC 28677
888-846-7567
www.thorlo.com

Index